7/27/2012

P9-CDB-808

Raising
Financially
Confident
Kids

raising
financially
confident
kids

MARY HUNT

founder and publisher of *Debt-Proof Living®* newsletter

Revell

a division of Baker Publishing Group
Grand Rapids, Michigan

© 2012 by Mary Hunt

Published by Revell
a division of Baker Publishing Group
P.O. Box 6287, Grand Rapids, MI 49516-6287
www.revellbooks.com

Previously published in 1998 and 2006 under the title *Debt-Proof Your Kids*

Printed in the United States of America

All rights reserved. No part of this publication may be reproduced, stored in a retrieval system, or transmitted in any form or by any means—for example, electronic, photocopy, recording—without the prior written permission of the publisher. The only exception is brief quotations in printed reviews.

Library of Congress Cataloging-in-Publication Data
Hunt, Mary, 1948–
    Raising financially confident kids / Mary Hunt.
        p.   cm.
    Includes bibliographical references (p.   ) and index.
    ISBN 978-0-8007-2141-1 (pbk.)
        1. Children—Finance, Personal. 2. Finance, Personal. I. Title.
HG1799.H86 2012
332.0240083—dc23   2012008120

Scripture quotations are from the Contemporary English Version © 1991, 1992, 1995 by American Bible Society. Used by permission.

Published in association with the literary agency of The Steve Laube Agency, 5025 N. Central Ave., #635, Phoenix, Arizona 85012-1502.

The internet addresses, email addresses, and phone numbers in this book are accurate at the time of publication. They are provided as a resource. Baker Publishing Group does not endorse them or vouch for their content or permanence.

12   13   14   15   16   17   18   7   6   5   4   3   2   1

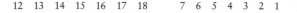

In keeping with biblical principles of creation stewardship, Baker Publishing Group advocates the responsible use of our natural resources. As a member of the Green Press Initiative, our company uses recycled paper when possible. The text paper of this book is composed in part of post-consumer waste.

Something amazing
happened on my way to getting
a financially confident life.
My kids got one too.

To my sons, Jeremy and Josh, in whose lives
debt-proofing was conceived and developed and continues
to be tested and found remarkably effective.
You've taught me enough to fill a book.
I love you forever.

contents

introduction

Something amazing happened on my way to getting a financially confident life. My kids got one too.

While our two boys, Jeremy and Josh, were still young, I awoke from a twelve-year spending coma to discover we were in the fast lane to financial ruin. I had done terribly with money and credit cards. Our situation brought new meaning to the term *debilitating debt*. We were in a horrible jam.

But even worse than the debt was this terrifying thought: What if our kids turn out like me? Were they learning from my behavior that they too were entitled to have what they wanted even when they didn't have the money to pay for it? Were they learning to worship money? Did they notice their mom trusting Visa and MasterCard more than she trusted their dad—her husband—to take care of the family? Did she really trust God the way she believed she was demonstrating to her children through her life?

Clearly, I was setting my kids up to become powerless pawns in the hands of an eager credit industry that is poised to enslave them to a lifetime of debt.

My husband, Harold, and I had so many hopes and dreams for our children—precious gifts we believed were given to us for only a while to care for, develop, train, and love and then to let go. If things didn't change, we were about to mess them up. Big time.

We had to find a way to teach our boys the truth about consumer debt and money. They had to learn that if they opened their lives to it, debt could prevent them from reaching their potential. Debt could negatively impact their adult relationships, diminish their options, ruin their futures, and destroy their dreams.

Debt prevention was what we wanted to achieve with our boys. But how do you do that with kids who don't even know what debt is?

It seemed to me that if we could teach our children not to touch a hot stove, we could train them not to get burned by the lure of credit-card debt. If we could train them to look both ways before crossing the street, we could teach them to carefully read the fine print. If we could instill in them the value of delaying gratification, that could become a lifetime behavior.

That's when we came up with the idea to "debt-proof" our boys by helping them develop financial intelligence, starting when they were quite young. Then when the time came, they would leave home with the skills, knowledge, and confidence to make wise financial decisions. We were on a mission to raise financially confident adults.

The following years proved to be remarkable in the Hunt home. I had a lot to learn and a huge financial mess to clean up. And the boys? They learned about personal finance right along with me.

Harold and I designed an aggressive, yet simple, kid-sized financial plan. In a nutshell, we assigned to each of our children a portion of the family's financial resources to manage, an amount commensurate with each son's age, needs, and ability. Yes, we handed over fairly large sums of money to their discretion and control. They had to go through basic training. They had rules to obey about giving and saving. They had expenses to cover, decisions to make, and consequences to suffer.

Because money management requires lots of responsibility, our boys learned the fundamentals of personal finance. They learned that to whom much is given much is required. Sure, they were just kids, but they weren't playacting—this was the real thing. And our kids rose to the occasion. Wow, did they rise!

If our plan to debt-proof our kids had been a miserable failure, you can be sure you wouldn't be holding this book in your hands. And had I known I would someday tell the story and offer the plan to you, I would've taken notes.

Thankfully, I have something better than notes or lesson plans. I have the living results in Jeremy and Josh. I am eager to let you get to know them better in the chapters that follow.

If I've learned anything from the stacks of mail I've received over the years, it's that kids—from all demographics—are leaving home and going into the real world knowing a lot of things. But money management is not one of them.

This is a chilling fact considering that the real world is where 90 percent of all divorces find their roots in financial disharmony;[1] where personal bankruptcy filings are on the rise every year, with 1.6 million new filings in 2010 alone;[2] where a $2.4-trillion consumer credit industry[3] is poised and ready to lure your unsuspecting young adult into its horrible pit of non-mortgage consumer debt. No doubt about it—what kids don't know about money can hurt them.

As parents, we make sure our kids get spiritual training, summer camp, and even private school. We enroll them in sports and expose them to music and computers to enrich, challenge, and develop them. We dole out wads of cash to make them good drivers. But a financial learner's permit? Hands-on money training? Judging from the heart-wrenching letters I'm receiving from parents, both single and married, I can tell you it's not happening.

Financial awareness shapes responsible kids. Teaching kids about money allows them to experience real-life situations and make real decisions and mistakes while within the safety net of their parents' care.

The debt-proofing process will make the adolescent years so much happier around your house. That's because the process builds a child's confidence and problem-solving abilities and makes basic mathematic skills more practical. It teaches values such as honesty, responsibility, generosity, and hard work. And this process of debt-proofing kids is gratifying for parents because the results are measurable and tangible.

Because money has such universal appeal, I've found that kids respond to it in similar ways, regardless of their temperaments or particular natural bents. Take my kids for instance. You could not find two more opposite people, unless, of course, you consider their parents.

Jeremy is gregarious, goal-oriented, excited, and, shall we say, controlling. Josh, our procrastinator, on the other hand, is calm, relaxed, and easygoing. But as different as they are in personality and temperament, when given the opportunity to manage money and make their own decisions, both became responsible and confident in all areas of their lives—not just in finances. Jeremy jumped right in and took control. Josh was less sure in the beginning and asked for advice along the way. But in the end, our plan produced the same result even though our subjects were and continue to be very different.

I'm stopping short of saying that teaching your kids about personal finance and the pitfalls of consumer debt will guarantee them lives of ease. I can't promise that, but I will predict that if you make a concerted effort to teach your kids about money and debt, they will walk into an adult financial world with the abilities they need to hold their own.

No matter your level of financial confidence, the amount of debt you may be carrying, or the mistakes you have made in your own life, teaching kids about money management is easy. Even if your own financial house could use a bit of tidying, you can start right away to debt-proof your kids. You will learn in the process.

I introduce this concept of raising financially confident kids to you as a friend, not an expert. I didn't breeze through the child-rearing years, believe me! Parenting is difficult work and probably the most challenging job I've faced in my life to date. Even though our boys are now adults, they will always be our kids and we their parents, which means we will always be learning. We didn't do everything perfectly by any means, but we did discover some amazing things that I believe will be of tremendous value to you and your family.

And now it's only fair that I warn you: When it comes to consumer debt, I am seriously opinionated. And on the topic of children—my own children in particular—I am unspeakably passionate.

My plan is that by the time you finish the final chapter of this book you will be keenly aware of the danger debt poses to the future of your children. But more than that, you will be ready, willing, and able to prepare them to face that danger as financially confident adults.

Let's get going!

1

developing financial confidence

Your kids are fortunate to be growing up in this progressive time in history. That's the good news. The bad news is that the very culture that offers them the world is also perpetrating a huge lie: You are entitled to have everything you want even if you don't have the money to pay for it. It's not a problem—just charge it!

The consumer-credit industry eagerly waits to fund that lie for your kids. They plan to give your children their very own credit cards—personal passports to the abyss of consumer debt—at the earliest age possible.

While the CARD Act of 2009 put a few restrictions on credit-card issuers who go after kids before they reach the age of twenty-one[1] (the youngster must have a cosigner or show proof of income sufficient to repay any debt), issuers are reportedly getting around this small inconvenience by allowing underage college students to count the proceeds of their student loans as qualifying income. And even though companies can no longer set up shop right on campus, pre-approved offers for credit cards with hefty credit limits are flowing freely to campus mailboxes.

Without preemptive intervention (debt-proofing), this could be the beginning of the end of all the hopes and dreams you have for your children's futures.

Do I mean to scare you? You bet I do. I feel like a flag man standing along the highway frantically waving you down. I'm begging you to stop and listen because there's serious danger ahead. You won't have to turn back, but I need to show you the detour.

They're Being Prepped

Your children are developing into world-class consumers. They are well on their way to becoming future debtors. The preparation is going on every day of the week, nearly every hour of the day.

Your children are being manipulated to think and respond according to the desires and agenda of the advertising and consumer-credit industries. But the influence is so smooth and subtle that I wouldn't be surprised if you're unaware of it.

According to iMediaConnection, a marketing trade association, marketing aimed at kids reaches up to four thousand messages per day. A two-year-old can recognize over two hundred brand names. Brand preference begins to show up at three years of age.[2]

If your kids read magazines, go to school, watch television, listen to the radio, know what a fast-food restaurant is, or have ever been inside a store or supermarket, I can guarantee they know about entitlement and instant gratification. They probably don't know those words, but they are learning the behaviors.

(Now before you slam this book closed because of what you assume is coming, relax. I'm not going to suggest you throw out the television or ban the mall. Together we're going to debt-proof your kids, not turn them into isolationists.)

Let me give you an example of consumer manipulation. Perhaps you are familiar with a campaign of television commercials for MasterCard.[3] The "priceless" ads capitalize on the value of human relationships. They're packed with emotion—the kind of productions that stir the soul. Each ad concludes with some variation on the theme that some things in life are "priceless," but for everything else there's MasterCard.

Now think about that for a minute. You and I know that's not really true—MasterCard doesn't provide us with everything money can buy. But the sentiment makes us feel warm and fuzzy about MasterCard.

What about your children? Take your eight-year-old daughter, who, by the way, is the age at which children are very literal. This is what she hears: Everything money can buy is yours when you have a credit card.

Multiply that kind of message by at least a million, and you'll begin to comprehend what a child is exposed to in this country before he or she reaches the age of eighteen. If a teenager lacks parents who educate and are role models to the contrary, we really shouldn't be surprised when that teenager finally gets a MasterCard and proceeds to do with it exactly what she's been programmed to do—use it to acquire all those things money can buy.

Here's the bottom line. Your children are being seduced by the consumer-credit industry to believe in and fall for the buy-now, pay-later lifestyle. If you do nothing to intervene, statistics indicate that your child is headed for a life that will be severely impacted by consumer debt.

The Problem

I have spent many years analyzing the trouble I got into with consumer debt. What in the world was I thinking? How could I have been so stupid? I've talked with thousands of people who were, and many who still are, in the same boat. I've also read letters from countless others with similar debt-related experiences. I have discovered three common characteristics in nearly every one of these depressing debt stories and disastrous situations, including my own.

Think of this as the recipe for making an explosive. Take a financially ignorant person, add attitudes of entitlement, and expose him or her to the availability of credit. Ka-boom!

The result is a situation so lethal that it has the potential of interrupting educations, wrecking relationships, ruining marriages, blowing families apart, destroying careers, and preventing joy and happiness.

The Antidote

The first step to debt-proofing your kids is to make a conscious decision to do whatever is necessary to teach and train them about money and the role it should play in their lives. Teaching your children the values and life skills they will need to live in the real world is one of your most important jobs as a parent. For better or for worse, money is the connective tissue that holds society together. It is not optional. We must have money to live. Your kids will need money to live. The only options you have are to address the issue or simply sit back and hope for the best.

The second step in this debt-proofing process is to learn what you're up against. Our society has odd values about materialism, consumerism, entitlement, credit, debt, and money. If you do nothing to counteract the destructive values the world wants to teach your kids, they are going to pick up the world's view very quickly. In chapters 8 and 9, you will learn what the consumer-credit industry has in mind for your kids and why. Unless you intervene now, their futures will be in jeopardy.

In the chapters that follow, you'll meet my family and learn about the unconventional family financial plan we developed in part due to the influence of Uncle Harvey. You'll find out everything about the plan, how we implemented it, and why debt-proofing was actually quite easy.

Teaching our kids about money by appointing them family money managers improved and enhanced our lives immeasurably. The absence of money conflicts between us and our kids allowed us to really enjoy our lives as a family—especially the adolescent years. In chapters 11 through 13, you will learn how to develop your own unique debt-proofing plan to:

1. tear down attitudes of entitlement
2. develop financial intelligence
3. neutralize the glamour of easy spending

That's what debt-proofing is all about. It's a specific plan to accomplish these three goals, and it uses money as the tool.

Ideally, your kids are young and you'll begin debt-proofing right away. Sooner is better. But let me assure you that no matter the age of your children, as long as they are under your influence and receiving your financial support, it's not too late. There are steps you can take to play catch-up.

Even if your financial situation is not so great, you can still debt-proof your kids. Even if you know nothing about personal finance, don't worry. Do not miss the opportunity you have to develop financial responsibility in your children. No one loves and cares about your kids more than you do, which makes you their ideal teacher. Thankfully, teaching teaches the teacher.

I've been where you are. I've experienced all of those feelings of inadequacy and personal failure. I know what it feels like to be scared out of your wits about the enormity and awesomeness of being a parent. And guess what? In spite of ourselves, our fears, and our inadequacies, Harold and I debt-proofed our kids.

Let me tell you about it.

2

what if my kids turn out like me?

I thought I knew plenty about parenting. Jeremy, born in 1974, and Josh, who completed our family some seventeen months later, proved me wrong. Seriously wrong.

I didn't know I could feel such love and care so deeply. I had read about maternal instincts and how one's life changes dramatically upon the birth of children, but nothing could have prepared me for the new level of emotions I experienced.

Without warning, some kind of Super Mom power hit me squarely in the heart. It filled me with amazing resolve: I will do anything to protect, prepare, and provide for our boys. My children will not experience pain, fear, or want. I will run ahead of them to smooth out all of life's rough spots. I was smitten and desperately in love with my children.

Caught up in the enormity of my new role as a mother, I didn't notice the way my own childhood had begun oozing into my consciousness.

Not a Typical Child

My parents considered me a difficult child, but not because I was particularly strong-willed or in poor health. I cried all the time and for no apparent reason. Not angry or defiant, I was a child with a broken heart. I spent most of my first seven years weeping. What on earth caused such pain? I couldn't explain it then and I don't know now.

A dark cloud of sadness followed me through my early childhood. My irrational fears only complicated the matter. The more I tried to be brave and not cry, the worse my problem became.

I often felt lost. No one knew what to do for me, and that left me to deal with the problem on my own. I hated feeling sad and wanted more than anything to be happy.

At a young age, I invented a secret way to make myself happy. I fantasized that I was rich. In the beginning, my daydreams were simply a coping mechanism to get me through the worst times. Dreaming, however, soon turned to goal-setting. I planned how happy I would be when I grew up and became wealthy. After all, I reasoned, we're poor and I'm sad. If I can be rich, then I'll be happy. While that is terribly flawed thinking for an adult, to a child's mind it made perfect sense.

My Plan to Be Happy

I practiced feeling rich by poring over the Sears catalog. Lists of all the things I would buy became my secret treasures. I would go up and down the aisles of the neighborhood store mentally filling shopping carts with everything that suited my fancy. I discovered I could will myself to be happy.

In time, I learned to control my weeping, much to the relief of my embarrassed family. I found success in school, loved music, and became a fairly decent pianist. But through all the years of progress and seasons of growth, the dark clouds only parted. The sadness would go away for a while, but my plan did not fade. Someday I would be rich.

Testing the Theory

I arrived at college with great expectations and mixed emotions. Scared to death but hopeful, I knew this would be the beginning of the rest—and the best—of my life. I planned it that way.

I had spent my entire life preparing for this new chapter. Convinced that real happiness comes through money and things, I finally had a chance to test my theory.

With a campus job and a checkbook, I could make my own financial decisions. I could buy what I wanted. When my wants exceeded my account balance, I learned the meaning of deficit spending through creative check-writing antics. If I could spend money, it felt as if I had money.

One happy moment after another, I could banish the recurring sadness quickly and effectively, albeit temporarily. I felt such freedom and control. In time, my happy days outnumbered the sad ones, and life was good.

Harold and I married soon after I graduated. Neither of

us could have imagined how the emotional baggage I brought to the marriage would affect our future.

I created in my mind an image of what our lives would be. Driving a certain type of car, wearing the right clothes, living in a certain kind of home were very important to me. We didn't have the income to support my vision in full. However, if we displayed signs of wealth and leisure, I could fool myself into thinking they were a true reflection.

Always on the lookout for signs of success, I hungered for statements that would confirm I was reaching my childhood goal. It didn't matter where the validation came from—a clerk in a department store was fine. If I could imagine this salesperson wishing she could be me instead of having to work behind that counter, I felt some weird sense of satisfaction. To receive a compliment on something I wore or a glance of approval for the car I drove was like a booster shot. Spending flattered, enhanced, and defined me.

Eventually, we moved to living the faux life, consuming as if we had a big bank balance. Consumer credit granted us a lifestyle we wanted but couldn't afford. Recklessly living beyond our means became our way of life.

Our New Life as Parents

Knowing we were about to become parents for the first time, we thought it appropriate to evaluate where we were and where we planned to go. We did not take lightly the awesome responsibility we would soon accept. Much to my discomfort, our finances were at the top of the list of things we needed to discuss.

During the first four years of our marriage, I had spent with selfish abandon and no thought for the future. We definitely needed a financial overhaul. But the timing wasn't ideal. Quitting my job dealt a severe blow to our income. We had just purchased our first home, and that brought new meaning to the matter of household expenses.

Naturally, there were things we needed for the new baby. (Little did we know how soon that would be "babies.") In the face of increased expenses, decreased income, and a pregnant woman's out-of-whack hormones, discussing our financial situation was more than I cared to face. So we didn't.

Confident of the safety net we had in available credit, we did what we had done so many times in the past: We pushed the subject to the back burner. We had a more important issue that would soon require our full attention. We would have plenty of time in the future to straighten out our finances.

Doing What Comes Naturally

Faced with the overwhelming task of perfectly parenting two precious, adorable sons, we did what came naturally. We overindulged them.

From their infancy I found personal satisfaction whenever I pumped everything money and credit could buy into our boys' lives. In some odd way, as I provided and cared for them, I was providing and caring for myself. I discovered I could relive my childhood through them. It was my chance to go back and fix things.

Instead of only dreaming of all the things in the catalogs or fantasizing up one aisle and down the other, I could make my fantasies come true. And since my efforts were not technically for myself but for my children, purchasing became a more noble act. Self-indulgence became self-sacrifice. Who could possibly find fault in these selfless acts of a mother providing for her children?

When I gave Jeremy and Josh what they wanted, it meant a double thrill for me. First I enjoyed their pleasure, and then I vicariously enjoyed it as I re-created my childhood.

I could give and do for them the things I had wanted at their age. If it made them happy, it made me happy. I liked that feeling. I found more pleasure in buying for my kids than for Harold or myself. And when I could surprise them with something they had not even thought of yet, it was better than Christmas.

I wanted Jeremy and Josh to have wonderful childhood memories, so I made sure they had everything they wanted, things their friends had—even things their friends could only dream of having. They participated in a full range of activities, attended the best schools, played sports, and wore all the right clothes.

The boys' competitions and assignments became my challenges. I wanted them to be winners—whether it was the AWANA Club's Pinewood Derby or the Great Americans Day speech contest. I made sure our Little League teams had the prizewinning banners and snacks to beat all. I couldn't fix the scores, and that's the only reason we didn't go to the World Series every season.

The sense that we had only one shot at their childhoods at times overwhelmed me. We had to get it right. I didn't care if that meant using credit to achieve success.

Harold would become agitated when I overspent, increasing our debt. But how else could I achieve my agenda of giving my children privileged childhoods? My stock justification for overspending on the boys: Debt is a small price to pay. How could anyone put a price tag on childhood memories?

Spinning Out of Control

Things began to turn sour when the boys reached school age. What began as a mother gifting her appreciative children had become children expecting too much.

In spite of all I did to please them—in truth, I was the one in need of pleasure—we watched in dismay as our adorable children turned into acquisitive ingrates. I worried the day was fast approaching when nothing would satisfy them and more would never be enough, for them or for me.

In other areas of life, we were diligently teaching our children important values of responsibility, honesty, self-discipline, and faith. But failing so miserably in this matter of personal finance—allowing our children to observe my inappropriate handling of money and credit and all that goes along with that—had the effect of canceling those other important life lessons.

After years of overindulging our boys, there was no way to ignore that things were spinning out of control. The more our kids had, the more they wanted. Demanding attitudes replaced childhood desires. What was cute on toddlers turned ugly on preschoolers. The more we gave, the less they appreciated. Jeremy and Josh felt entitled because they believed their parents had unlimited cash resources. To my shame I had taught them well.

I made sure Jeremy and Josh felt entitled to all the things they wanted but became outraged and embarrassed when they became active participants. I fed my need for material gratification by bringing them surprises and buying them what they wanted at every opportunity. But when the boys greeted me—and everyone who came to the door—demanding, "What did you bring me?" my reactions were not cute or adorable. How dare these children of mine act so presumptuously?

Birthday party invitations became a battle just waiting to happen. It was nothing for one of the boys to insist on a sixty-dollar toy for his friend's birthday party. A parent-child fight in the toy store is not a pretty sight. But uglier than the battle (won by the parent, by the way) was what I knew it meant. They wanted to be the best liked at the party, to be the most popular, to impress their peers. They wanted everyone to think they were rich. They needed a gift with a big price tag to prove it.

I tried to ignore the conflict I felt.

I Don't Do Money

The Southern California economy was hot in the late 1970s. There was no end in sight for the unprecedented rate our home was appreciating. I didn't know exactly how it worked—I didn't do money. But the growing equity was my justification for living without limit. We'll just pay off everything later, I reasoned. That kind of fuzzy thinking justified reckless spending. It felt good to impress my kids with our bogus lifestyle. I needed them to think we were rich, but more than that, I needed to believe it myself.

When Jeremy was eight and Josh seven, I finally faced our financial reality. Credit abuse, debt, and terrible money management had led us on the path to financial ruin. Yet even though we were in a horrible jam, we successfully shielded our kids from the sordid details. Harold left his banking career at my pleading, and we headed for the greener pastures of self-employment. Not a good idea.

During this horrible season of our lives, a terrifying thought kept running through my mind: What if the boys turn out like me? Clearly, they had learned from my behavior that they, too, deserved to have what they wanted even when they didn't have the money to pay for it. But were they learning to worship money? Did they overhear their parents arguing about money? Were they feeling the terror that gripped my soul, knowing our family was in danger of imploding?

I didn't like the cold, hard truth, but I knew my children were on their way to living their adult lives as we were—riddled with debt. I was pointing the way and giving them detailed lessons by allowing them to observe and imitate my behavior.

I taught them by example that when you don't have enough money, you don't have to stop spending. I used credit to build a bridge between what we made and what we wanted. And when the canyon grew wider? I just built a bigger bridge.

The Bridge Collapses

In 1982, my life crashed at my feet. We lost our business, and an avalanche of debt was ready to bury us. I feared I would lose the only things that really mattered—my husband, our kids, and our home.

Completely broken, I confessed to God that the manipulation, the scheming, the deceit, and the lying were sin. I begged for his forgiveness and promised to do anything necessary to pay back all the debt. Determined to change my ways, I vowed to find my security in God's promise to provide for our needs.

The charade of appearing rich to my kids, to myself, and to the world slowly disappeared in the light of this new reality. I finally stopped living in my financial fantasies and decided to begin making progress in repaying debt, reducing expenses, and living beneath our means.

As I became willing to change, God made changes possible. As we became willing to be good stewards of what God had given us, he brought amazing opportunities our way.

We were in the beginning stage of what would be a thirteen-year period of financial recovery. Clearly, it was time to make significant changes in the ways we were training our children regarding money and things. We had to stop reacting to their insatiable demands and desires. Those out-of-control attitudes of entitlement I'd created had to go.

It must have been a confusing time for the boys. While they were not privy to the hideous details of our financial condition, they couldn't help noticing we were saying no more often than yes. Kids are intuitive—they knew I was going through a time of what I called personal growth. Fair or not, things changed as if overnight. We went from spending as if there would be no tomorrow to finding every way possible not to spend money—and without much explanation.

We knew Jeremy and Josh desperately needed to learn the lesson that "money doesn't grow on trees." But how?

We needed a great plan with an easy-to-follow road map. The kids weren't getting any younger, and we had no time to spare.

3

meet uncle harvey

I saw Uncle Harvey only three times, but I felt as if I had known him all my life. That's because I knew the story.

Uncle Harvey gave each of his four sons an entire year's worth of money at the start of each new year. No weekly allowances, no paying for haircuts, clothes, or school expenses. Uncle Harvey flat-out gave them all the money they would need for the entire year.

All at once. In cash.

The ground rules were simple: Everything, beyond food and shelter, that cost money became each boy's own financial responsibility. There was a huge expectation that they would manage their money well. Uncle Harvey's annual caution was, "And if you run out, don't come crying to me."

Uncle Harvey wasn't actually my uncle but rather my husband's. The significant age difference between my husband, Harold, and the cousins (Harvey's boys were much older), together with the fact that we lived thousands of miles apart, meant I only heard about this family. Everything I knew I learned from relatives. But what I learned, I really liked. This unconventional parenting technique fascinated me.

Reports of how this arrangement panned out were always amusing. As the stories went, one of the boys was quite a skinflint. He refused to spend foolishly and was even reluctant to spend his money on necessities like shoes or clothes, a quirk that brought a bit of embarrassment to his mother, Aunt Rotha.

Another son spent wildly and with reckless abandon. Invariably, he had to get a job come February or March. Even though he initially had lots of trouble making his money last, eventually he got the hang of it.

What really impressed me was how Harvey's plan worked equally well with each of his boys. It didn't matter that they had diverse personalities and abilities, that they were as different as day and night. Harvey and Rotha used money as a tool to train their boys regardless of each son's individual characteristics, tendencies, and abilities. And their hands-off policy encouraged the boys to become innovative and creative. Each son was compelled to create some kind of financial plan, a plan that fit him uniquely.

I played the scene over and over in my head. It was so fascinating to me how Uncle Harvey, a tall, thin man of few words, would call the family together each New Year's Day. He would slowly reach into his pocket and pull out a pile of cash. Very deliberately and without a word, he would divide the cash into four piles and look each son straight in the eye as he handed him his annual portion of the family's financial resources. Uncle Harvey was the kind of man who commanded your respect.

Oh, how I wished I could have been a fly on the wall during just one of those uncommon funding events. Everything about it—the passing of values from parent to child, the unspoken demand put on these young boys to reach to the very limits of their abilities, the tough yet tender way Uncle Harvey demonstrated how much he cared for and trusted his boys to make wise and thoughtful decisions—always moved me.

And how did it all work out? All four boys became responsible and highly capable businessmen. Each of them married for keeps, and to my knowledge, each continues to possess uncommon financial acumen. I could draw just one conclusion from all of this: Uncle Harvey was on to something!

Harold and I often talked about the amazing Uncle Harvey and what a clever man he was. There was something remarkable about the way he encouraged his boys to reach their maximum potential.

Uncle Harvey was himself a successful businessman, so of course there had to be more to this story than a man showing up once a year to hand money to his kids. He must have been an example from the day they were born. Surely they observed their father's faith, integrity, and business sense in action. When their father spoke, they listened—and they learned.

How could anyone not see the association between the end products—four decent, successful men—and the unconventional way they were raised?

I made the connection and carefully tucked it into the back of my mind. I didn't think about it again until years later when we had two boys of our own.

4

a plan to call our own

remembering Uncle Harvey's money plan was like finding a long-lost treasure. It had hope written all over it.

Harold and I didn't recall Harvey's plan in exactly the same way—it had been more than ten years since the subject had even come up. But that didn't matter. We needed the principles, not the details.

Was there any way we could incorporate those principles into a plan for our family? That was the big question. Clearly, we couldn't duplicate Harvey's strategy. For starters, we didn't have a year's worth of income lying around. Our situation was worlds apart from that of Uncle Harvey and Aunt Rotha. We could, however, use Harvey's basic plan as a model to design our own finance plan—a specific strategy that would fit our unique situation. And so with Uncle Harvey as our inspiration, we set out to design a customized financial blueprint for our children.

Over the next few months, planning took priority. We made sure our sessions were top secret. We knew the element of surprise would play a key role in the launch. Whatever we came up with, it couldn't be just another blip on the screen of our children's lives. It had to be significant and life changing.

Harold and I had been through some tough times in the previous years. Our willingness to communicate openly had taken a beating, and we were working diligently to strengthen our relationship. Now as we united our minds in developing a plan, our hearts knit together more tightly because of our intense love for our children and concern for their futures. Our common goal became our common joy.

It took time, but we eventually came up with a plan that had all the elements necessary for our family and our situation. Our plan was not long or complicated. It was so simple that even a child could fully understand it. The following was our basic outline.

The Financially Confident Kid Plan

Mission Statement

1. To develop our children into effective money managers.
2. To educate our children and steer them away from consumer debt in an effort to protect their futures.
3. To gradually turn over to our children the money required for their care and support as members of our family.

4. To trust them to be good stewards of a portion of the family resources.
5. To adapt the financial training of our children so it is in keeping with their God-given characteristics and tendencies so that when they come to maturity they won't depart from the training they have received.

Commencement Date

Each child in the Hunt family will enter the plan on the first day of sixth grade.

Salary

While in the plan, the child will receive a monthly "salary" that will become his to manage. The amount of the salary will be determined by the parents. The salary will be subject to annual review by the parents or more often as deemed necessary. The salary will be increased on the first day of each new school year commensurate with parental discretion and according to the child's demonstrated ability to be an effective and wise financial manager.

Mandatory Disbursement

The child must give away 10 percent of the total salary. He must save or invest 10 percent in a real bank or other parent-approved investment vehicle. The balance of the monthly salary will be used according to the child's discretion in keeping with the family's values.

Responsibility List

The child will receive a list of items and activities the parents will no longer pay for while the child is receiving a monthly salary. The list is subject to review and revision at any time by the parents. Additional items will be added to the list on the first day of each new school year commensurate with the increase in salary.

Hands-off Attitude

The parents will not criticize or interfere with the child's management decisions as long as the child follows the rules and demonstrates his ability to live and to manage his salary according to the family's values.

Filling in the Details

Each year we would increase the boys' salaries and add more items to their lists. Every year we would release to them greater levels of responsibility. Our intention was that by their senior year in high school our boys would be managing all of the money they required—everything except the basics of shelter and food consumed while at home. These expenses would include clothing, school, personal hygiene, transportation, dating, sports, and church activities.

Knowing that our job as parents is to take care of and then let go of our children, we would issue them wings one year at a time. Our hope was that "flying lessons" from a young age would provide them with the confidence and expertise they would need to take their solo flights from the nest at the appropriate time.

There was nothing magical about our commencement date—the first day of sixth grade. That happened to be the time in Jeremy's life—our first program participant—when we came up with our plan. In hindsight, I now believe age ten or eleven is the ideal time to start such a plan, for reasons we will discuss in later chapters.

We purposely avoided the word *allowance* because it was too familiar. Some of our kids' friends got allowances. We'd given Jeremy and Josh an allowance occasionally, but it had no clear meaning. There was no expectation or guidance—and none of us knew when they'd get it again.

Quite frankly, we didn't want to reeducate the boys about something we'd already tried or deal with comparisons to what other families were doing. We wanted something fresh that would grab our kids' interest and command their respect. We wanted our plan to be so unique that Jeremy and Josh would sit up and take notice. The term *salary* seemed to fit the bill on all counts.

Graduation Day

Deciding how our plan should end was an important detail we failed to address in the beginning. Developing forever-parental-salary-dependent children was not our intent.

The purpose of this plan was to prepare Jeremy and Josh to become self-supportive for life. We had to be careful not to coddle them into the unrealistic expectation that the real world includes free lunch.

After much discussion, Harold and I decided our responsibility to support our children financially would continue through the summer following high school graduation. This would allow three months for them to replace their salaries with real jobs or suffer the consequences. If they found jobs before the three months were up, they'd still receive their salary. Perhaps the prospect of a double-dip would nudge them toward independence sooner rather than later. Several years later we added the following to our plan: Children will graduate from the plan three months following high school graduation, at which time their salary will cease.

We had no intention of kicking the boys out of the house when their participation expired, only that their salary would cease. As family members, they could still live under our roof and eat our food. Beyond that, they'd be on their own. Hopefully, college would follow.

Determining the Salary

Designing the basic plan wasn't as difficult as filling in the details. What would be a fair monthly salary for an eleven-year-old boy? What level of financial responsibility should we give? Our boys were very different (and remain so to this day). Would they require customized plans? What would work for Josh might not work with Jeremy. We wanted to turn over the maximum amount of money possible that would be in keeping with the abilities, age, and stage of each boy's life at the time he entered the plan.

We wanted to stretch their minds and deliver a clear message of how much we trusted them to live their lives according to our values and to make our values their own. Whatever amount of money we chose would have to be enough to last for an entire month but could not be so much to preclude the necessity for thrift and careful management.

At the same time, I was finally learning the benefits of living more frugally. It was becoming more important to us that our kids learn these lessons much sooner than I had. We leaned heavily on the truth that kids learn and adapt much more easily than adults.

All the plans in the world couldn't change the fact that we weren't in a financial position to add new expenses to our lives. Our desire was simply to redirect money we were already spending. For instance, if we gave Jeremy a total of five dollars over the month to play video games in the past, then in the future we would give him the five dollars all at once. Then he could dole it out to himself rather than taking it from us twenty-five cents at a time.

The time to decide on a salary for Jeremy (our first participant) was approaching in just a few months. We needed specific information, and our memories weren't very reliable. We weren't expert managers and didn't know where all our money was going.

Take the infamous video games, for example. I estimated we gave Jeremy two dollars a month for video games. Harold thought it was more. Beyond that minor expenditure, how much did we fork out in a typical month for school expenses and events, entertainment, snacks, comic books, and so on? We had to start keeping specific spending records. Thankfully, we had a few months before the official launch.

The results startled us, to say the least—nearly ten dollars for video games in a single month and four bucks to the man in the ice-cream truck. (Keep in mind that both boys are in their mid-thirties as I write; the dollar figures I quote reflect what things cost when they were about ten.) Then there were event tickets, various sports and school functions that required money, club dues, movies, skateboard paraphernalia, manuals and books, treats, comic books, birthday party gifts, and on and on. We were forever handing our kids money for one thing or another. They'd put out their hands, and somehow we'd manage to fund the current need or want.

Learning how much money we spent on our kids for non-essentials opened our eyes to a new truth. It was shocking, to be perfectly candid.

From the information we compiled, we determined Jeremy's beginning salary structure and first-year responsibility list. His salary would be fifty dollars a month for the first year. His responsibility list included optional childhood expenses such as video games, snacks, food away from home (unless it was part of a family outing), school lunches (if he decided not to take a sack lunch from home), treats from the ice-cream truck, birthday gifts for friends, comic books (Jeremy was an avid collector), hobbies (he'd developed a rather pricey interest in skateboarding), school supplies, movies, school events, and so forth.

We included a "miscellaneous" category on his list to cover anything that might come up from time to time that we would determine to be optional. Kids are very literal, and we knew

Jeremy would find every loophole if any existed. We added this just-in-case provision to keep us from being painted into a corner by a very clever child.

We determined that with a monthly salary of fifty dollars, by the time he gave and saved, he would have forty dollars to manage. That seemed about right.

Our salary plan did not represent a new household expense. It was the money we would have spent on our children anyway.

If we gave Jeremy fifty dollars a month in salary, it wasn't as if we had to come up with an additional fifty dollars each month to fund a new obligation. The truth is that we were probably spending more in an average month—we really didn't know for sure because we'd had no reliable accounting system.

For years the money had simply dribbled out of our pockets into the hands of store owners and ice-cream truck drivers. It "ka-chinged" its way into video game coin slots one quarter at a time (remember, this was pre-home-computer-game days, before kids had cell phones, text messaging, and all manner of other pay-to-play opportunities) and was handed out bit by bit for school functions, birthday parties, mall trips, and grocery store treats.

Designed to gather myriad child-related expenses into one tidy sum, our plan would change the ownership from Mommy and Daddy's money to Jeremy's money and Josh's money. That idea alone had a significant benefit. As long as the money was seen as parental funds, there was no limit, no apparent end to the resources. Transferring the salary to the boys inherently created budgetary limits.

As citizens of the household, both boys did chores commensurate with their ages and abilities. We increased their chores as they got older. However, we decided that chores would be separate from payment of their salaries.

Dealing with Infractions

No plan is a good plan without a provision for how to handle infractions. We had to come up with consequences if the boys disobeyed or failed to follow the rules of the plan.

Deducting from their salaries as a punishment for wrongdoing would be one way to handle infractions. But that didn't seem to meet our desire to make the boys more self-governing. Our purpose in all of this was to prepare them for real life. We wanted the way we treated infractions to be more reflective of life in the real world.

When adults break the rules, they suffer consequences that are not directly salary related. For example, if you get a speeding ticket, the courts don't call your employer and instruct that the cost of the ticket be withheld from your next paycheck. Your speeding ticket and paycheck are not directly related. Instead, if you get a big fat speeding ticket, it becomes your responsibility to see that it is paid—not your employer's.

Taking our cues from what the boys could expect once they entered the real world, we adopted a citation program. Failure to complete chores or other violations of our rules would result in stiff fines. Citations would be issued with a due date, and then it would be up to the boys to pay their fines within that time frame or suffer even greater consequences, such as losing privileges or temporarily giving up favorite toys and possessions. Our goal in attempting to emulate real life in this way was to teach the boys how consequences play out in the real world.

On paper the plan looked great. We had the first salary structure and responsibility list in place. We were hopeful.

But would it work?

5

ready, set, launch!

during the weeks before unveiling the plan to the boys, I came down with the equivalent of buyer's remorse. Were the rules too rigid? Were we offering too much too soon? What if an obsession with money drove our sons to become greedy little Ebenezer Scrooges? Or what if this crazy idea backfired and did nothing more than fuel the entitlement attitudes they had already begun to exhibit?

Our boys weren't rebellious, and they had a healthy respect for our authority. However, we weren't out of the woods when it came to ugly attitudes of entitlement.

In hindsight, I know it wasn't their response I feared or the plan I doubted. Harold and I were confident we had a plan that Uncle Harvey would approve. While it wasn't as clear to me then as it is now, my apprehension was due to what this would cost me. This plan required that I begin letting go—not a pleasant thought for an overly controlling parent.

We unveiled the plan to the boys during the summer before Jeremy entered sixth grade. We explained how he would start first and Josh would follow in two years. We presented the plan with great fanfare. This was a big deal for our family—the start of an important season of life, a formal rite of passage. We started with a general overview and followed later with the details.

The fact that Jeremy's beginning monthly salary would be fifty dollars—more cash than either boy had ever seen at one time—was the pièce de résistance. We had his attention and that of his little brother, Josh, who settled into the role of spectator.

First We Give

We described to Jeremy all the ways he could handle the mandatory giving rule. He could give to a friend whose parents were out of work, a needy person he might meet, a special project at school, the church offering. The decision was completely up to him, provided he gave thoughtfully (a good steward takes responsibility), without strings attached (once he gave he couldn't demand anything in return), and faithfully.

His questions provided perfect teaching moments. Naturally, he wanted to know if we gave 10 percent of our money and to whom. We had great conversations. We explained that God asks us to give back to him part of everything we receive. We told him we gave our money to God through the church offering. But Jeremy would have to make his decision based on what he decided was the right thing for him. He should pray and ask God for wisdom about where he should give his money.

We explained that giving money to a guy on the street corner with a "will work for food" sign would qualify but could be a little risky. Is this guy legitimately needy? Will he use the money wisely? Perhaps a more responsible way to help homeless people would be for him to give his money to the rescue mission because they know the best way to use the money. Taking responsibility is the mark of a good money manager, we told him. The rest of the lesson is that once you make the decision, you give and then it's hands-off. A gift with strings attached is no gift at all.

Then We Save

Next we presented the mandatory saving rule. Before he spent any of his salary, he had to save 10 percent. Our family now obeys this rule of life: You always save part of everything you get, so you are never broke.

Money when saved earns interest, which makes it grow. Interest is money that goes to work for you, and just like seeds you plant in the ground, it grows and produces more money. The word *withdrawal* didn't cross our lips. We must have taught with great authority because Jeremy didn't ask how to get the money out. By inference we told him you save it forever.

We made a trip to the bank in our neighborhood to open a school savings account (a special account for a child in which the parent is a cosigner and there are no fees or minimums imposed). We picked up a supply of deposit slips, practiced filling them out, stood in line, and met a teller. We even checked the counter height to make sure our first participant could complete his transactions without assistance.

With Freedom Comes Responsibility

Next came the list. We spent many of our training sessions talking about all the things in our lives—and Jeremy's—that cost money. We went over the responsibility list and how it would grow each year, requiring greater accountability. We explained that once he entered the plan, Jeremy would be making his own financial decisions regarding those things on the list.

My memory says that Jeremy's first-year list included video games, treats from the ice-cream truck, all school expenses other than tuition that we considered optional, skateboard paraphernalia, comic books, snacks away from home, gifts for birthday parties, social events, and related expenses—in short, everything we considered optional and for which we'd given him spending money in the past.

Amazingly, Jeremy never questioned any part of the plan. He welcomed everything we told him and accepted it as if it were the law of the land. That to me was confirmation of an important fact: Children want boundaries. They crave the security that limits and clear expectations convey.

Boot Camp

In the following weeks, we explored many scenarios. "If we go out to eat pizza with friends (a typical family occasion for us), you'll have to remember to bring your own quarters if you intend to play video games." "If you are invited to a friend's birthday party and you choose to attend, you'll be responsible to pay for the gift." (Finally, a way to stop those parent-child birthday gift battles and the ugly taste those wars left in our mouths.)

We discussed at length the consequences of making unwise choices. "If you forget to bring quarters to the pizza parlor Friday night, you won't get to play," or "If you bring all of your money and go nuts, you won't have any money for the rest of the month." "If you choose to buy an expensive gift for a friend's birthday, you'll have to say no to other things during the month. The choices you make will directly affect your life."

Jeremy's excitement was contagious to his little brother and added to the importance of his impending rite of passage. Surprisingly, Josh didn't ask for special treatment. He didn't beg for an early start. He fully accepted that he was younger and his time would come.

Along with the basic rules of the plan, we discussed with Jeremy how Christmas was four months away and he would have to start planning soon if he intended to buy gifts. We also tried to anticipate upcoming birthday parties for which he would need to prepare.

We went over the plan ad nauseam. We role-played, we quizzed, we concocted possible situations he might encounter once he became an official family money manager, and we posed trick questions. We went over the mandatory disbursement rules and drilled him on the characteristics of a good steward. We made charts showing how money grows when exposed to compound interest.

Jeremy's understanding and ability to process this information were amazing. He could respond with creative solutions to any challenge we posed. He knew the plan backward and forward, and there was no doubt—this kid was ready!

First Payday

On that first payday, Jeremy received his salary in cash—ten five-dollar bills. Just as we had rehearsed so many times in the preceding months, he put 10 percent into the giving envelope and took off for the bank with the five-dollar savings account deposit. This was about the easiest training we had ever done. He just "got it."

Jeremy knew his exact financial obligations in the coming month. While not a requirement, I suspect he made lists for how he would manage his newly found source of wealth. We felt great relief and even a hint of pride. After all, fifty dollars represented quite a risk to take on someone so young, so inexperienced.

6

meltdown on aisle 5!

Jeremy hadn't been home from the bank for more than five minutes when he asked to go to the toy store. What?! I panicked momentarily and then calmed down as I realized he must need to comparison shop for his brother's upcoming birthday or get a jump on that Christmas shopping.

We had drilled into Jeremy's head the idea of planning ahead. There was no way he could have selfish motives in mind! Sure, he had been one to feel entitled to anything he wanted, but we had cut him off at the pass. To eliminate attitudes of entitlement was the heart and soul of our plan—the reason we had just spent the better part of the summer preparing and training him.

To say the trip to Toys R Us was difficult would be a gross understatement. I had to bite my tongue to keep from blurting out, "What in the world is this all about, young man? Just exactly what are you planning to buy? How much money did you bring? Are you sure you remember everything we've talked about? I just knew you were too young to trust with this much responsibility. We should have known better. You're the oldest. You have to be a good example to Josh."

Internally, I lost control. Containing the frustration, disappointment, and anger wasn't easy.

I wish I'd had a video camera. Not only could I have captured this moment for posterity, but filming the scene would also have provided something constructive to take my mind off what was happening.

I don't know when I've seen such a fixated shopper as Jeremy that day. He was analyzing and comparing, but not for his brother's birthday or to get some early holiday shopping out of the way. Standing there in his favorite aisle—Star Wars—he might as well have been on the front porch of heaven.

We stood in that store for what seemed like an eternity. Harold and I could do little more than shake our heads and hope for the best. We had made a pact that we would not interfere, criticize, or in any way impede Jeremy's decisions regarding the discretionary portion of his salary. How would he learn if we weren't completely hands-off?

I don't recall what it was he bought that day, but it was some large thing he dreamed of owning. I realize now that he'd been making plans for this day all through basic training. He had been dreaming of how it would feel to be rich, the same dream I had had at his age.

Jeremy's purchase came to $39.92. The kid had 8 cents to his name to last for the rest of the month. I was mortified.

How could we have been so stupid? What did Uncle Harvey know that we didn't? We trusted in our plan to prevent this very thing. Jeremy knew better than that! He knew we had plans to go out for pizza with friends where video games would be the order of the evening. Surely he was old enough to know the difference between a quarter and eight cents. What was he thinking?

My mind was a blur of doubt and disappointment. What should we do? We hadn't discussed the subject of loans (there would be none, that's for sure), so he couldn't be thinking along those lines. How would we ever enforce such a strict austerity program for four long weeks? Eight cents doesn't go very far. Had he blatantly disobeyed? Should we treat this as open defiance? Should we cancel the plan, tell him he was a failure, threaten to never trust him again?

The trip home that day was long and miserable—but it paled in comparison to the month that followed.

Harold and I had many long discussions—the kind we'd never had before. We had always controlled the purse strings and in so doing tightly controlled our boys' lives. In the past, we had made all the decisions, often to our sons' loud objections. More often than not we would give in and then kick ourselves. We hated feeling like the bad guys when we had to say no. But that wasn't any worse than giving in with a reluctant yes and then realizing once again how we over-indulged our kids.

After a great deal of discussion, we made the very difficult decision to stick by our plan and keep our mouths shut. We wouldn't mention the purchase either negatively or positively.

We also decided to be silent regarding the obvious state of poverty into which Jeremy had placed himself.

During that first month, Jeremy gave away the five dollars in the giving envelope (by his choice he put it in the Sunday school offering). He might have thought about a savings withdrawal but did not mention or act on it. He missed out on many things. He sat while others played video games (a very big deal to him at the time—hardly anyone had home versions then), he missed a birthday party, and he suffered. But not once did he whine or complain.

I, on the other hand, was miserable. I've never been big on watching my kids suffer, particularly if there was something I could do to stop it. But this time I had no choice. If our plan was going to have any hope of success, I had to get a grip.

With all the attention devoted to Jeremy's financial plight, I failed to notice how much money we didn't spend on him during the month I thought would never end. The pain of it all was over quickly, but not the valuable lessons.

Same Song, Second Month

The second month began the same as the first. We gave Jeremy his salary in ten five-dollar bills. He put 10 percent into the giving envelope and took off for the bank with five dollars for savings.

Apparently he'd become used to his self-imposed austerity program because he continued in that mode during the second month. Only the pendulum swung to the other extreme. We couldn't believe it.

As if overnight, he matured right before our very eyes. His frantic need to spend and accumulate was slipping away. A certain calmness and confidence settled in. It was nothing short of amazing.

Jeremy was invited to a birthday party during that second month. Another Toys R Us experience just waiting to happen? Not quite. Instead of requesting a ride to the toy store, he opted for the local supermarket. I'm sure every grocery store in the country has a rack that holds packages of cheap trinkets like plastic rings or rubber balls. I've always thought of these as disposable party favors—just one step above junk. No doubt Jeremy had viewed that rack from his perch in a shopping cart many years before because he knew exactly where it was. Clearly, he had a plan in mind. How could we fault him since that is exactly what we had been teaching him to do?

The gift he selected for his friend's birthday was—you guessed it—one of those favor-type packages. I stood there feeling the same shock I'd felt the month before as he blew all of his disposable income on himself in one fell swoop. I wanted to scream, "A one-dollar gift for a friend's birthday party? Are you out of your mind? What will everyone think of you? Worse, what will they think of me? You can't do this! This is your friend. You have to spend at least what he spent on you!"

If I had to bite my tongue in the toy store the month before, this time I was drawing blood. Surely the calmness I'd been feeling was the storm's precursor: I wasn't up to this adventure.

But in my most casual of manners, I asked Jeremy if this was what he really wanted to give his friend. He explained that one dollar was the amount he could afford and that it was a really cool toy.

Everything in me wanted to stop this nonsense immediately. I wanted to take control and get things back to normal. But I couldn't. We'd talked about not giving up if the going got rough, about making difficult choices and then living with the consequences. I knew memories of the party and the chintzy gift would fade in a few days, but these lessons would shape Jeremy's financial future. How could I even think about quitting? To criticize his financial decision would be to stomp on this young seedling whose financial roots were just starting to take hold.

The second month was as spend-free as the previous one had been caution-free. One time during that month when faced with a video game opportunity, Jeremy played two games and stopped. The rest of the time he watched as others fed quarters into the machines. He'd planned to spend only two quarters and that's exactly what he did. No complaints, no whining. Right before our eyes, a quarter, a dime, a five-dollar bill were taking on a whole new meaning for this kid.

Remarkably, changes were going on inside me too. I was beginning to experience something I'd heard about but had never known firsthand: Teaching teaches the teacher. All of us were focusing on spending decisions and the importance of planning and prioritizing. I became more aware of my spending decisions and began looking for even better ways to avoid unnecessary purchases.

Harold and I didn't confront Jeremy about the spending choices he made during those early months. Instead, we found opportunities in the regular flow of life to talk generally with Jeremy about how the choices we make affect our lives. When we make bad choices, we have to live with them. Sometimes unwise choices take away options. We used ourselves as examples, sharing with him tidbits from our lives that were appropriate for him to know.

Because Jeremy chose to spend all of his money on himself that first month, he severely limited his options for the rest of the month. The consequences were fairly benign in the larger scope of things, but to an eleven-year-old boy they were devastating—a situation he would never repeat. I don't believe there was any other way we could have taught that lesson. All the lecturing, role-playing, practicing, talking, or modeling could not have accomplished what real life did.

Jeremy had to test the system and then suffer the consequences. Learning this lesson early, while the consequences were minimal and over the safety net of our care, made a lot of sense. Imagine if he had experienced this kind of freedom for the first time away from home, on a college campus, with a $5,000 spending limit on a credit card with his name on it. One month would have been all the time needed to plunge his life into a downward spiral.

As the months went by, our "Jeremy pendulum" settled down to a gentle, consistent ticking one might expect from a finely tuned clock. His insatiable appetite for stuff quieted, and his spending became well thought out and deliberate.

I'm sure he made an occasional bad choice with his money

in the years that followed, but none of us remember. There really was no way he could make any huge mistakes because there was no opportunity for debt. He could never spend all of his money. The plan acted like guardrails to keep him from going over the edge.

Here Comes Josh

It was fun to watch younger son Josh observing older brother Jeremy during those first two years. With Josh we continued the status quo, keeping the purse strings tightly closed. We would give him a buck or two now and then for spending money but paid for everything as we had in the past. We wanted to retain a clear differentiation between a plan member and a nonmember, which was Josh's status. Amazingly, this child, who had such difficulty learning and for whom development was a challenge, understood quite well his brother's privileged position of being "on salary."

For two years he was like a kid with his nose pressed against the window of the candy store waiting for it to open. He was content in knowing that on a very special day—the first day of grade six—he too would become a full-fledged family money manager complete with a salary.

Josh learned more from watching his brother than we could have ever taught him. Practically speaking, he entered the plan the same day Jeremy did, only he sat on the bench. He learned from Jeremy's mistakes and accomplishments, and his private comments to me were priceless. "Can you believe Jeremy did that?" or, "He did really good this month, huh, Mom?"

Not once during those years did Josh complain that he couldn't participate, nor did he ask for us to bend the rules so he could get off the bench and into the game earlier.

Josh's rite of passage occurred on schedule. We made a big deal about his first day of sixth grade, but this was such familiar territory that it seemed almost anticlimactic. With plenty of time to watch and plan his opening moves, he was eager to begin, and we were eager to watch his actions.

Because Josh had shown the tendency to be a bit of a spendthrift in previous years, Harold and I assumed that when his pendulum stopped swinging so wildly, he'd settle down to become our spender son, where Jeremy had become the saver.

To our delight and surprise, Josh set a very conservative pace from the start and thrived in the structure and expectation of our plan. No questions, no fumbles, no excuses.

There aren't stories to tell of Josh's financial escapades or foolish choices. He took to the program in textbook fashion, one financially responsible month after another. Yawn.

Year after Year

On the first day of each school year, salaries were increased and responsibility lists expanded. We kept turning over more and more money plus more and more responsibility to our kids. They thought they were getting these fabulous raises, but in truth we were simply allowing them to hold the money we would have spent on them anyway. If this were a company, we were the executives, delegating fiscal authority over a portion of the company's assets.

As each boy hit the second year, we added clothing upgrades to their lists. This meant that while we would still pay for their clothes, now there would be spending limits. For example, we would pay $25 for shoes twice a year. If we found shoes for less, we benefited from the good deal—we did not rebate the difference to the boy.

If one of the boys decided only $195 big-name sneakers would do, fine. He had to come up with the $170 difference, also known as an upgrade. It's amazing how that simple technique can take sneakers from nothing-else-will-do to really-kind-of-stupid in about three and a half minutes.

Prior to the advent of the Financially Confident Kid Plan, Jeremy was bent on a special brand of clothes. In his mind, there was no allowable substitute. I'll admit it—I thought it was cute how this little guy was so loyal to a particular brand. Once we added the upgrade feature to the responsibility list, however, brand loyalty lost its glamour.

At some point, shoes were totally added to the responsibility list, which moved them into the area of essentials. Because of the nature of the plan (the boys had full discretion over 80 percent of their salary), the boys had the choice either to buy shoes or not. Don't worry—our boys never went without shoes, and neither will yours. They may not have always worn the shoes I would have selected, but that doesn't matter now. What matters are the lessons they learned, the parental trust they enjoyed, and the maturity they demonstrated. Sure, they made some regrettable choices. But their decisions didn't harm them; they taught them to make better choices the next time. They learned that the cheapest shoes aren't always the most comfortable, and if you are patient, the better ones do go on sale sooner or later.

Early on, both boys started saving more than 10 percent. Their savings accounts became a significant part of their lives, and they learned by experience that spending is fun but fleeting, while the joy derived from saving goes on and on.

They saved a significant part of their salaries, they saved their birthday money, they saved gifts of money received at other times during the year. When they earned money from odd jobs and summer endeavors, they saved.

When they turned sixteen, we finally introduced the concept of the savings withdrawal, and both boys bought their first cars with the money they had saved.

That these kids could accumulate that much money amazed all of us. They proved to themselves from a young age that five dollars here, two dollars there, a little bit today, and some more tomorrow adds up significantly. And the decision whether to spend or save—beyond the mandatory rule—was completely at their discretion. The requirement was to save 10 percent, but many months they saved 80 percent and lived on 10 percent.

According to plan, both boys opened checking accounts in their high school senior years. While we didn't monitor any of their banking activities beyond teaching them how to reconcile their accounts, to my knowledge, neither Jeremy nor Josh bounced a check. In fact, neither could imagine how anyone could be that stupid—to write a check for more than they have in the bank.

Both Jeremy and Josh have become checkbook resistant adults—a trait I highly respect. Given my history with checking accounts, I was worried about how they would do with one. Thankfully, both boys prefer to live with cash and write checks only when absolutely necessary.

No News? Good News!

At this point one might expect to read about all the financial mistakes the boys made and how we, their brilliant parents, turned those experiences into lifelong lessons. I'm nearly embarrassed to report that when it came to money, the years were quite uneventful. The plan went as designed. The fact that we had a plan communicated a sense of fairness to the boys. If that's what the plan said, that's what we did. Even though we made adjustments along the way, there wasn't a sense that we were making up the rules as we went along. When there was a question, the plan supplied the answer.

The teenage years were the best years of all. We were free to enjoy our kids and they us. We didn't experience the parent-child conflicts that arise because of money pressures that we observed in families around us. The boys didn't ask for or expect gas money or funds to cover this school event or that social occasion. They had their salaries to manage. There were no discussions about annual car registrations or who would pay for other expenses. Money was simply not an issue.

Just as planned, both boys reached maximum salary and maximum responsibility in their high school senior years. By then they were managing all of their expenses as frugal consumers. They saved far more than they spent and did not demonstrate compulsive behaviors. But beyond that they were profoundly responsible, not only with money but also with their lives as a whole. Those were delightful years.

Multiple Benefits

While designed to benefit our kids, we now realize how much the plan benefited us, their parents. We consistently spent less on our kids than other families with similar circumstances because we had built-in spending controls. Our family's giving was consistent and our savings level was high. The boys' salaries became a fixed monthly expense we could plan on in the same way we could plan on our mortgage payment. We had our spending plan, the boys had theirs. It was a beautiful thing.

Dividing the management of our household income among all members of the family was a brilliant idea. But, of course, we couldn't take credit for it. It did, after all, originate with Uncle Harvey.

7

parenting—a curious profession

Parenting has to be one of the most important if not most challenging jobs in the entire universe. Yet, it requires no license or degree—not even an entrance exam. And just when you learn the ropes and get really good at it, your job up and leaves home without you.

I have been a parent for a lot longer than I wasn't one, a small piece of trivia that recently piqued my curiosity and sent me in search of a calculator.

As long as we're talking about jobs and professions, consider this: The typical worker in the US puts in 40 hours a week, 50 weeks a year, for a total of 2,000 hours annually.

As a mom I've clocked 168 hours a week, 52 weeks a year (motherhood knows no vacation), or 8,736 hours a year. I have completed 37 years or 323,232 hours on the job. Now, by applying the 2,000-hour-per-year standard, I have logged the equivalent of 161 work years as a parent.

My time on the job and a couple of terrific children may not qualify me as an expert, but they have given me a wonderful opportunity to discover some effective and dependable principles that work to equip kids with the values and financial skills they will need in the real world.

The Most Critical Part

It's easy to get so hung up on the mundane side of parenting—cooking, cleaning, carpooling—that we forget about the single most important job parents have to do: successfully pass on our values to our children.

Equipping children with values is not the same as making them obey rules. Parents can get a kid—even the dog—to do just about anything, provided they exert enough external pressure. Threats of severe consequences motivate immediate compliance but aren't likely to produce long-term commitment. When the child or teenager is free of the external pressure, his behavior reflects his true values—the condition of his heart, his authentic character.

Kids who leave home having never taken ownership of positive values, such as integrity, responsibility, courage, and respect, don't make the transition into the real world very well. They bounce around and make all kinds of foolish choices. Often they suffer long-term consequences simply because they do not have a positive, strong value system. They have nothing to guide their lives.

Passing to your children the values and financial skills they will need to prosper in the real world is the very heart and soul of debt-proofing—values having to do with the right way to manage money and how to live without debt.

One of the most exciting and gratifying aspects of parenthood is to watch as children assimilate positive values having to do with money, credit, and debt. Even at relatively young ages, they will begin to accept responsibility for their choices and behavior. They choose to do the right thing simply because it is right, not to escape external pressure or to earn a reward.

Persuasive Parenting

Suppose a couple wants to impress upon their daughter that lying is wrong. A strong, clear threat ("It's bad to lie, honey, so if I catch you at it I'll cut your tongue out") might well be effective when the parents are present or when the girl thinks she can be discovered.

However, it will not achieve the larger goal of convincing her that she does not want to lie because she thinks it's wrong. To do that, a much subtler approach is required. A reason must be given that is just strong enough to get her to be truthful most of the time but is not so strong that she sees it as the obvious reason for her truthfulness.

It's a tricky business because this barely sufficient reason changes from child to child. For one child, a simple appeal may be enough ("It's bad to lie, honey, so I hope you won't do it"); for another, it may be necessary to add a somewhat stronger reason (". . . because if you do I'll be disappointed in you"); and for a third child, a mild form of warning may be required as well (": . . . and I'll probably have to do something I don't want to do").

Wise parents will know which kind of reason will work on their own children. The important thing is to use a reason that will initially produce the desired behavior and will, at the same time, allow a child to take personal responsibility for that behavior. And the less outside pressure necessary, the better. Selecting just the right reason is not an easy task for parents, but the effort should pay off. It is likely to mean the difference between short-lived compliance and long-term commitment.

As Samuel Butler wrote more than three hundred years ago, "He who agrees against his will is of the same opinion still."

Basic Money Values

Values are specific types of beliefs that are so important and central to one's life that they act as life guides. Values are central to a person's personality and are responsible for motivations and important decisions that have far-reaching implications. Behavior is the outward expression of one's values.

Debt-proofed kids are guided by a set of values having to do with money, credit, and debt. The parents of debt-proofed kids should be guided by these values too.

I've discovered that most adults don't have a specific value system when it comes to money management, so debt-proofing your kids may well have an added bonus for you.

Here are four simple but extremely powerful basic financial values that are part of our family's value system. They are the values we passed on to our children through this process I call debt-proofing. They are so simple that even a child can learn and understand them but so powerful that accepting them as life guides can turn even the most difficult financial situation around.

Giving

The first part of everything that comes into my life is mine to give back. I give because I am thankful. Giving proves the condition of my heart. It's a thank-you note for all that I am and all that I have.

Saving

I always save part of my money and earn interest on it. It is wrong to spend all of my money and not save some to grow for the future.

Spending

I do not spend more money than I have. I decide if something is a want or a need. If I spend all of my money today, I won't have any for tomorrow. I shop wisely. I buy only what I planned on, not what's on the display.

Borrowing

I always avoid borrowing money. If I cannot avoid it, I borrow only for things that gain in value and only when I give collateral. I repay my secured debts as quickly as possible. It's wrong to carry unsecured debt.

Know Your Child

Do you ever feel like what you say to your kids just bounces off their foreheads? That what you tell them just isn't getting through?

That happens to all of us from time to time, but some parents never manage to get through to their kids because they've never truly connected with their children's hearts. They just keep piling on external pressure. Then the kids leave home and completely abandon everything their parents "taught" them.

Children throw off external parental pressures the minute they escape the strong arm of authority. If all those lessons and lectures haven't penetrated their hearts and become part of their value system, they'll leave home without them.

Parents need to establish a strong and dependable connection with their kids' hearts. I like to think of it as a channel for communication, the channel through which to deliver life-guiding values. The way to build this all-important channel is to know your child.

It is possible to live under the same roof with people who eat your food and have the same name without ever really knowing them. It happens all the time.

Parents give birth, have a preconceived blueprint of their dream child, and get so busy raising Wonder Child according to their design and to fit their dreams that they never really know who this person is.

74

Many homes are filled with cookie-cutter kids. They are treated exactly the same way. They receive the same training and the same discipline, and they're expected to turn out the same way: perfect.

Charles Swindoll, in his book *You and Your Child*, says, "You cannot discipline a child you do not love. You cannot love a child you do not know. You cannot know a child if you are not sensitive."[1] Wow! Read that through a few times and let it soak in.

I believe that every child is a unique creation. Your child is unlike anyone in your family or anywhere on earth. Everything he or she is or can become is all there, wrapped up in that tiny bundle.

To realize that your child was born complete with individual characteristics, abilities, and talents is not just awesome—it takes a lot of the pressure off you to come up with a superior design. God has already taken care of that!

My Life as a Piano Teacher

I taught piano lessons to children of all ages for about ten years. With a top enrollment of about seventy students, I had many opportunities to observe all kinds of parents. I had dominant parents, permissive parents, elective parents, and, thankfully, many loving-yet-firm parents.

Dominant parents were my least favorite. They were rigid and controlling. Because they decided their child was to become a concert pianist, it was my job to make it happen. They didn't care that there might be other considerations. Like talent. They believed that enough discipline, willpower, and determination could change a baseball player into a Beethoven or a bookworm into a Bach.

I could tell within a few sessions if a child had any natural ability. Those students who had talent always did well. They loved to practice and were eager to learn. I couldn't wait for their lessons to see the progress.

Then there were my talentless kids who showed up each week only because their parents yanked them from their sports or computers to take these stupid piano lessons. They were as miserable being taught as I was teaching them.

Who wants to be crammed into a mold that doesn't fit? Who likes to participate through force in something that offers little hope of success? I couldn't help but observe the interaction between these children and their parents. The child's spirit was closed tighter than tight while the angry parents tried to pry their way in. I don't like to think about it, but there is the possibility that something as minor and inconsequential as piano lessons built walls of resentment that have yet to be torn down.

Author Gary Smalley, in his book *The Key to Your Child's Heart*, explains that the dominant parent has very high standards and expectations for a child. This type of parent tends to be unbending and demands strict adherence to a list of rules.[2] According to Smalley, rigid dominance breaks the spirit of a child and results in resistance, clamming up, or rebellion. In the end, the child usually rejects his parents' rules and their values.

Think Gardening

Parents should take lessons from people who love to garden. Gardeners are kind and gentle, patient and nurturing. No matter how dirty they get, they just keep cultivating and encouraging. Only a completely ignorant gardener would ever take a rosebush and attempt to turn it into a pine tree.

Imagine a gardener gets a seed. That's it. Just a tiny, helpless, needy seed. All she knows is that it's one of a kind and more precious than gold. Should she give it full sun? Or partial shade? Keep it moist or allow it to dry out between watering? What type of fertilizer? Pest control? Without an instruction manual, the gardener won't have those answers until she gets to know this unique gift.

First, she allows the seed to sprout—not out in the cold, harsh world but in the warmth and shelter of her care. With each day she gains more insight into what she has until she determines the characteristics of this tiny seedling. She studies what great gardeners before her have written about this particular type of seedling. She seeks advice from experts. She is driven to discover the exact conditions the seed needs for optimum development.

As the seedling gets stronger, the gardener begins to expose it to a variety of conditions that will encourage and develop its natural strengths. The gardener tends to it every day. She doesn't let it grow wild but instead supports and trains it to grow into the shape that most becomes its natural characteristics.

She feeds it with just the right combination of nutrients and fertilizer. She talks to it and encourages every tiny new shoot.

This treasure is her pride, her joy, not because she created it but because it was a gift that she cared for and nurtured to its full beauty and potential.

Values Are More Often Caught than Taught

Bents, characteristics, abilities, and tendencies are the conduits through which you can pass your values to your children.

But exactly how do you make the pass? Through your life. The way you live. Kids learn most effectively through observation and imitation. It's the witness of our lives, more than anything we say, that is taken in slowly and cumulatively by our children.

Children drink in everything around them. They see the way we act with others. They listen to everything we say. They observe the way we handle our money. They hear what we say on the telephone and the way we deal with salespeople. Children compare what they see with what they are told, and in the case of a clear conflict, they usually go with what they see.

There are many ways to communicate your values to your kids. There are formal lectures, specific talks, books and discussions of what has been read, reprimands, reminders, various kinds of discipline and punishment, and religious education with all of its related activities.

All of these ways of communicating with your kids do count for a great deal, but they cannot come close to the value of your children observing their parents living out their values consistently, specifically, and diligently day in and day out. That's the surest way to pass on to your kids the values and principles they need to guide their lives—values that will take root in their hearts, not simply stick on the outside until they can get away from your authority.

This Is Not New

The importance of passing on values and important information to the next generation is not a new concept. An excellent example can be found in the Old Testament.

It was almost time for the people of Israel to cross the Jordan River and conquer Canaan, but God refused to let Moses lead them into the land. Instead, Moses had been told that he was going to die on the eastern side of the Jordan. So Moses gave several farewell speeches to the people of Israel in which he repeated many of God's laws.

Moses also reminded the Israelites about the past forty years. God had rescued them from Egypt and taken care of them in the desert, but they hadn't always been faithful or obedient to him.

Moses told the Israelites that if they kept their agreement to worship and obey the Lord, they would be a successful and powerful nation. But if they broke their agreement and worshiped idols, the Lord promised to put terrible curses on the people. They would be defeated by their enemies and lose their land and their lives.

You can tell just how important it was that they pass on the laws to the coming generations by the way Moses instructed them to do it:

Memorize these laws and think about them. Write down copies and tie them to your wrists and your foreheads to help you obey them. Teach them to your children. Talk about them all the time—whether you're at home or walking along the road or going to bed at night, or getting up in the morning. Write them on the door frames of your homes and on your town gates. (Deut. 11:18–20)

Read that account again, but this time think about your kids and this matter of passing on to them financial values of debt-proofing.

First, memorize the four basic money values in this chapter. Make copies of them (you can skip the wrist and forehead action). At the appropriate time, teach them to your children. Talk about them all the time as the subject fits naturally in your family life—when you're at home or walking in the park, when you tuck the kids into bed, and when they get up in the morning.

But most importantly, let your kids catch you in the act of living those values!

8

they're coming after your kids

They're big, they're powerful, and your kids are in their crosshairs. Credit-card companies are desperate for new customers, and they have their big guns pointed at your children.

Only forty or so years ago everyone paid for almost everything with cash. Remember that? Consumer credit was unheard of.

Early credit cards such as Carte Blanche and Diner's Club had a certain snob appeal because only the very elite qualified to have one. For the average person, paying for things with credit was rare—something our grandparents would have never considered. Back then no homeowner in his right mind would have thought of applying for a second mortgage to pay a few bills and treat the family to the vacation of a lifetime.

Consumer credit has changed the way people live and think. Today credit cards are accepted as payment for everything from groceries to utilities, taxes to charitable donations, post-age stamps to automobiles. And where banks used to be careful to make sure a person did not become overextended with credit limits, nowadays the more debt a person has, the more credit he gets.

US consumer debt recently reached $2.45 trillion, more than double what it was in 1996, according to data released by the Federal Reserve Board in September 2011.[1] This period has seen an unprecedented boom in the consumption of goods and services that help make our lives easier, and more fun. But it has also created a society that has become nearly addicted to having what it wants when it wants with little thought for how to pay for it.

Credit cards have made it possible for the typical American family to live beyond its means. The average credit-card debt per household with credit-card debt currently stands at $15,799.[2] Paying only the minimum payment each month keeps more than 60 percent of all cardholders in "perma-debt," a state most families have come to accept as normal.[3]

One of the hottest prospective markets for new credit customers is the next generation of spenders—our kids. While the marketing tactics are often subtle, the industry pursues our kids with a vengeance. They're counting heavily on a new generation of debtors who will carry on the consumer-credit tradition. These marketers are making a serious effort to get children to believe that credit cards are good, that it's okay to pay with plastic if you don't have the cash.

America's kids are becoming increasingly accepting of plastic, finding it far friendlier than cash. And why not? Cash makes you think. Plastic is so easy. Kids see their parents living on plastic, so why shouldn't they live that way too?

They're Coming after Your College Students

Back in the late 1980s, when credit-card companies saw they were running out of new customers—the adult market was saturated with nearly half a billion credit cards—they began looking for greener pastures.[4] They decided to take a chance on college campuses. The idea was a bit risky. After all, who ever heard of unemployed teenagers being able to qualify for credit? To their amazement and fiscal joy, not only was the grass on the other side greener, but college campuses turned out to be pure gold.

Colleges have come to rely heavily on the "rebates" they receive from credit cards issued on their campuses. They agree to affinity cards with the college logo on them. They benefit financially every time the cardholder makes a purchase with that particular card. In 2010, credit-card issuers paid colleges $73,261,906 in accordance with the various college credit-card agreements, information cited in the Federal Reserve Board of Governors Report to the Congress on College Credit Card Agreements, July 2011.[5]

Even with the regulations of the CARD Act of 2009 now fully in place, it's not at all unusual for preapproved credit-card applications to find their way into student mailboxes, stuffed to capacity with plenty of tempting offers.

I spoke with the dean of students of a prestigious private university who reported that they don't allow credit-card companies to set up shop. However, they cannot censor the US mail, and so the credit-card companies simply flood the campus with preapproved applications in this alternative way.

Check out this new card "invitation" that showed up in the mailbox of Kelly, a young college-bound Floridian. I hope you're sitting down.

"Free from parental rule at last! Now all you need is money. Cha-Ching!" (envelope copy). Inside is a lengthy, convincing marketing piece that reads in part:

> Getting the credit you need to get through college is easier than you'd think. In fact, it's almost a no-brainer. Just send in the invitation above or give us a call. If you qualify the Associates Visa card will be in your mailbox before you know it. Get 3 percent cash back on everything you buy. Just imagine, 3 percent cash back on living expenses, text books—everything you buy with your Associates Visa including pizza! How cool is that? All you have to do is carry a balance from statement to statement and keep your account in good standing and you can get 3 percent cash back on all your net purchases. Just think how much college costs these days, then figure out how much a 3 percent rebate would add up to. That's some serious cash!

Who but a credit-card company would advise a young student to carry a balance from month to month? At this card's annual interest rate of 17.99 percent, the cost of this "deal" is still 15 percent—a hefty rate.

By the way, the fine print sheds a little light on that 3 percent rebate that's supposed to be so terrific. The maximum Kelly could earn in a year is just $100, which is subject to all kinds of conditions and exclusions, including "the terms and conditions of this rebate program may be changed or canceled at any time and for any reason."[6] In other words, many purchases may not qualify for this overrated rebate.

I'm happy to report that Kelly turned down this offer, but if she'd fallen for it, she would have had to charge $3,300 in qualifying purchases (a nebulous term without clear explanation on the application) and pay 17.99 percent interest on the revolving balance to get that $100 annual rebate. I would hardly call that "some serious cash." But some serious debt? Oh yes!

Often credit-card solicitations come with emotion-packed messages. Jeremy received his first one in the spring of his senior year of high school. It read something like this:

> You're going to college. You'll be away from home for the first time. You'll experience all kinds of new things. Some will be fun and exciting, but chances are you will encounter dangers like car trouble or other emergencies. There will be books and basic living essentials. Your parents won't be there to help. Let us be there to take care of all these unexpected expenses.

Clearly, this solicitation was designed to move the terrified college-bound student to action with a one-size-fits-all solution for grown-up situations. I can understand how a financially ignorant, frightened teen could fall for this false notion that credit is the antidote for all of life's problems.

According to Sallie Mae's 2009 study on undergraduate credit-card usage, the average graduating college senior leaves school with $4,100 in credit-card debt on top of $23,200 in student-loan debt.[7]

You may wonder how credit-card companies can justify extending that kind of credit to unemployed students. They play the odds. They know that most college students have parents or other family members supporting them in some way. They bank on the fact that most parents, no matter how angry or disappointed, will come to the aid of their children when they get into trouble. And they have also discovered that students who have been bailed out by Mom and Dad are excellent risks for new cards, because if parents will rescue them once, they're likely to do it again.

There's lots of competition these days between credit-card companies, and that's what drives the marketing campaigns. Card companies want to establish a long-term relationship. They want to be the card that gets carried in the wallet for many years.

One Loyola Marymount student I met years ago had a story that still sends chills up my spine. Granted, I met him pre-CARD Act of 2009, but given that he was older than twenty-one, the current age limitations would not have prevented his activities.

It seems he was fairly impressed with his ability to get credit cards. He had barely unpacked his bags at school before he started filling out the credit-card applications. He got plenty—seven cards in all.

He bought designer clothes, stereo and electronic equipment, and computers—plus all the fancy meals and concerts he and his friends could possibly endure. His high living gained him more friends than he knew what to do with. In less than five months, even before the second semester of his freshman year, he had maxed out the cards to the tune of $25,000.

But did he worry? Of course not. He knew his parents would eventually find out, get really mad, and then get over it. He was partly right. They did find out. And they got really mad. But they didn't get over it. And they didn't bail him out.

He had no choice but to drop out of school and give up his scholarship. By the time I met him on the set of a talk show, he'd been working full-time for quite a while. He said he hoped to go back to school someday when he got the credit cards paid off and his life together.

In a letter I received, Maureen wrote, "When I went to college I couldn't believe all the credit-card applications in my mailbox. I even got a gold card with a $7,000 limit. I charged it to the limit in a matter of months."[8]

Like Maureen, most teens have never learned the dangers of unsecured credit. They leave home financially ignorant, clueless how credit cards work. So when they find out they can break free from parental rule by helping themselves to all they would like from the campus credit-card smorgasbord, they comply willingly. Conventional thinking makes the attractive spending limits look like "free money," so why not?

Cyd recalls how the myth of free money impacted her life. "My first credit card arrived just days after my twentieth birthday. I was so delighted.

"Getting a card was so easy. I felt so grown up—no longer a teenager. I was living in an apartment and now had the power to go shopping whenever I wanted. I could finally get some decent clothes for work, finish furnishing our apartment, and on and on. Never mind the fact I had to take a second part-time job to afford my share of the expenses and quit college so I'd have time for my two jobs.

"My Visa led to many store credit cards and oh, so much more spending power. I couldn't believe that I could get so much (a two-hundred-dollar spending limit on a store card) for so little (only ten dollars a month . . . that's all?). Adulthood was wonderful."[9]

The pervasive attitude among college students when it comes to credit cards is spend now, worry later. Their futures look rosy, and immature wisdom says, "When I get out of school, I'll get a great job and pay it all back really fast." Of course, that's exactly the way the credit-card companies want them to think. But statistics prove otherwise.

That's what Kay believed. "I'm twenty-three years old, and currently my husband and I are twenty-five thousand dollars in debt, not including our mortgage. I went off to college, and one by one the credit-card offers poured into my mailbox. I applied for several and of course received them all.

"By the time I got out of college I had seven cards and twenty thousand dollars' worth of debt. That's more than I paid for my entire college education. I bought stereos, TVs, clothes, food, a computer, furniture—all the things I thought I needed. I figured I would pay it all off when I graduated and got a good job.

"Well, today I have graduated and have a good job, but my entire check is currently going to pay off my debt. Even with an aggressive repayment plan, it's still going to take over three years to get out from under this horrible load of debt. We want desperately to start a family, but we've had to put that dream on hold because of the debt.

"It would be easy to blame my parents for my problems because they never taught me how to manage money. But the truth is they didn't know either. They often got themselves into impossible situations with consumer debt and had to be rescued by relatives. Never once was I warned about the dangers of credit or taught how to save, give, invest, and manage my money."[10]

When students graduate from college, reality sets in. Their first assignment as an adult is to figure out how they're going to repay their student loans, juggle huge credit-card debts, and cover "incidentals" such as rent and transportation.

Unlike any generation before, those coming out of college nowadays aren't simply broke. They're in the hole with significant debt and ruined credit ratings. What a way to start out!

Consider this letter I received from one Texas Tech student. "I ran up seventeen thousand dollars in debt by my junior year, dropped out of college, and filed for bankruptcy."[11] Tragic.

Not all students get so mired in credit-card debt that they have to drop out of school. But current trends suggest that those students who overextend themselves with credit-card and student-loan debt during their college years are setting themselves up for failure once they leave school.

The CARD Act that took effect in February 2009 places limitations on the ability of credit-card companies to offer accounts and credit limits to students under the age of twenty-one, which could lead us to believe that the days of college student credit-card-debt horror stories are over. But that would be a mistake.

Despite the CARD Act, college students are still being heavily targeted by credit-card companies. According to a recent survey of college students by the University of Houston Law Center, 76 percent of those surveyed under age twenty-one said they had received a credit-card offer since the beginning of 2010, and 73 percent of freshmen say they saw credit-card issuers marketing to students off campus. As for the income requirement, 29 percent claimed their student loans as part of the income they reported to the credit-card companies in order to get the cards.[12]

With so many loopholes in the CARD Act, credit-card companies still have easy access to young consumers under age twenty-one.

They're Coming after Your High Schoolers

High school? No way!

That was my reaction when I began getting letters from readers of my Debt-Proof Living newsletter telling me their high school kids were getting credit-card applications in the mail. I was skeptical. Somehow a kid's name had been mixed up with the parent's. It had to be a mistake. Sure, I'd read plenty of news stories about pet owners receiving preapproved offers addressed to the family dog, but mostly those were flukes that gave us a lot of laughs.

But these letters I was receiving weren't jokes. Some readers even sent me the solicitations so I could see for myself that their high school children were indeed being targeted by credit-card companies. And there was no shortage of horror stories from parents whose kids signed up, unbeknownst to the parents, and proceeded to get into some serious financial hot water.

Thankfully, direct solicitation of credit cards to underage teens has stopped. The collective outrage from parents and the media did a lot to quell the practice, and the enactment of the CARD Act of 2009 made it unlawful.

But has this stopped the consumer-credit industry from coming after our children? No. It has only prompted them to change their method to one that is more subtle but equally compelling. They are targeting children by making payment by plastic the proper way to acquire things. From the moment a child is born, it seems, MasterCard and Visa are doing all they can to make themselves attractive to children, their logos as recognizable as the famous golden arches and their use as normal as—and highly preferable to—that of cash.

"Call it plastic on training wheels!" was the message in one press release for Discover's Current Card, a prepaid debit card aimed at "kids, tweens and teens."[13] The idea is that parents open this account with their child, then deposit money in the account. Now the kid takes possession of the card and uses it to buy stuff or make withdrawals from ATMs. Because it looks just like a credit card, this card makes your little darling feel so grown up—the perfect card for parents who want to give their teens some freedom. "Unlike cash," reads the press release, "the Current Card gives teens a better way to track and manage their spending while developing smart money-management skills."

I could fill several pages with all of the prepaid cards being offered, all of them carrying either the MasterCard or Visa logo, designed to look just like a credit card. But youngsters don't know to make a distinction. They don't fully understand that someone has to put money into the account from which they can withdraw funds to make this card work. To them it's magic. Want something? Swipe the card.

And can we talk about fees? They're high on these cards, and going higher if the banks have their way. Perhaps by the time you are reading this, per transaction fees for all debit-card transactions will be in full force.

Perhaps the worst thing about debit cards is that they encourage the user to overspend. It just doesn't feel like real money, so why worry about how much you're loading into the cart? Or how many times you download a $0.99 tune, ringtone, or game app? And that is by design. We know that people who use a debit card routinely spend 30 percent more than if they used cash.

As painful as it may be to part with cash, there's nothing more real to a kid than paying with cold, hard cash and taking a direct hit to the wallet at the moment of purchase. It's important for a child (even adults for that matter) to have the pleasure of the purchase immediately tempered by the pain of payment.

They're Coming after Your Youngsters

You probably think you've reached the comedy portion of this chapter, that I'm only kidding that the credit-card industry is interested in capturing the attention of your school-aged kids. Even your toddlers. It's not a joke, folks. I'm serious.

The consumer-credit industry won't be contacting your little ones through the mail. They know little kids can't read. But they know what all kids love. They've managed to make toys an inroad of choice to familiarize even the youngest members of your family with the idea of credit.

Little Tikes Cozy Pumper,[14] for little ones ages eighteen months to five years, is quite adorable. Toddlers quickly learn how to pump gas into toy cars. The fuel buttons make fun sounds when the kids stop to fill up. There's a hose with a pretend nozzle. But it doesn't stop there. It is outfitted with a credit card swipe and the child's own pretend credit card, which makes paying at the pump so easy and all too realistic.

I'm still shaking my head over Mattel's Cool Shoppin' Barbie and her realistic boutique play set. Barbie comes complete with a realistic MasterCard embedded in her hand, a larger one for the child, a cash register, and a credit-card reader that chirps "Thank You" and "Credit Approved!"[15]

Several years ago, the Store for Knowledge, in partnership with television's Public Broadcasting System, unveiled its alternatives for parents who had had it with violent video games and grinning fashion dolls. Most would assume that such an endorsement from PBS would have our children's best interests in mind. As far as I'm concerned, they should have looked a bit farther.

At the top of that year's list was the Pretend & Play Calculator Cash Register. Intended for children ages three and up, the solar-powered toy includes a toy credit card and features realistic sound effects. Of all the toys PBS presented to their test group of youngsters in an effort to determine the top ten educational toys, the cash register with the pretend credit card was the most popular. Since then it has won no fewer than nineteen awards.[16]

All three of these toys, with just a tiny tweak, could be terrific teaching tools for kids. The gas pump could come with a money slot and realistic currency. Cool Shoppin' Barbie could carry miniature wads of cash, and her little cash register could chirp "Cash sale! Congratulations, you're a smart shopper!" The solar-powered cash register could dump the credit card and contain just—imagine this—cash!

Sadly, toys like these send a message to children that credit cards are good and should be as much a part of their lives as cars, trucks, and baby dolls.

Not long ago I was standing in a checkout line behind a young woman and her daughter—a child who I'm guessing was about six years old. The woman put all of her purchases on the counter, and the sales clerk inquired as to the method of payment. The woman looked adoringly at the child, who was carrying a small plastic wallet, and encouraged her to answer the question. Without a word, the little girl opened the wallet to produce a real Visa card, which she handed to the clerk. The mother beamed as she handed the card back to her daughter so she could "take good care of it until we get to the next store."

I was mortified. And if you know me, you'll be surprised to know I didn't say a word. I even turned the other way, knowing I couldn't hide my bewilderment. Here was a child who will grow up assuming that plastic is the way to pay for all the things she wants.

They're Showing Up in the Classroom

Personal finance has become a widely mandated subject in schools. Forty-nine states have adopted economics curriculum standards, but only 38 of those have a personal finance element. Most school districts simply have no funding available for curriculum—and that provides the perfect situation for flawed and biased materials to slip into the classrooms of America.

Visa, in its "Practical Money Skills for Life" curriculum, states that it's fine to carry up to 20 percent of your net income in credit-card debt. The highly regarded nonprofit educational organization, Jump$tart Coalition, in its materials warns that credit is the way of life in America, and if you cannot get credit on your own, you need to get a cosigner. The group advises that people keep credit-card indebtedness under 20 percent of household income.[17]

Make sure you know exactly what your kids are learning about money in the classroom. The personal finance materials available in cash-strapped schools today are often compliments of companies that have a glaring conflict of interest. They are looking to influence youngsters to accept consumer debt as the all-American way of life. By all indications and most regrettably, it's working quite well.

Bad News, Good News

Consumer debt is one of the biggest killers of relationships, dreams, futures, and happiness. Over and over I've heard the stories of how it started innocently—usually in college or during the first years of marriage. While the circumstances are all different, the same theme comes through loud and clear.

"I had no idea what I was doing. I thought it was okay because they approved me. I didn't intend to go nuts. We got married, and because of our student loans and credit-card debts, we fought all the time, and now he's gone."

Here's a perfect example from a letter I received not long ago: "I am twenty-two and my husband is twenty-three. We are sixty thousand dollars in credit-card debt. I obtained my first credit card upon entering college and faithfully paid the entire balance each month until we got married.

"My husband received his first card at age fourteen when his mother applied in his name in an attempt to get new credit after a divorce destroyed her credit rating.

"His mother paid his balance, maintained his checkbook, and mostly took care of all the financial responsibilities. When he came to college he struggled with money. He didn't know so many credit cards existed and accepted every one.

"We graduated, quadrupled our income, and quadrupled our spending, of course. Then our student loans came due.

Things became tight overnight, but we still had plenty of money to cover the bills.

"My husband began seeing me as controlling and restrictive with money, not wise and trustworthy as I thought he should. I wanted us to live on a budget and start repaying debt quickly.

"Just a few weeks ago he asked me for a divorce. I had no idea he believed that was our only alternative.

"I know that money is not the only source of our problems, but how we spend it illuminates the differences in what we believe and how we conduct our lives. For my husband money represents freedom, control, and the right to live his life the way he chooses."[18]

Everything you've read so far in this chapter is the bad news. It's the ugly truth of what's out there waiting for your kids. Now here's the good news: You can intervene. Your kids, no matter their abilities, tendencies, or characteristics, can learn to say no to credit-card offers. I believe with all my heart that if kids learn the truth and the dangers of debt early in their lives, potential harm can be prevented.

Please hear me. There's a horrible stalker out there waiting for your kids. As things stand right now, your children are in great peril. They are being conditioned to believe that credit cards are the way to have everything they want and that carrying revolving debt is the way to live. But you can change that—you can do something about it.

It's not reasonable to think we can stop this stalker—the consumer-credit industry. Even if there were reasonable solutions, we don't have time to wait for new legislation, organize massive boycotts, or in some other way try to slay the dragon.

What is reasonable is that we can educate our kids. This stalker is only as strong as his prey is weak. Ignorance will keep your kids weak, but knowledge will fill them with power. If you teach children the truth about consumer credit and how to make wise financial decisions, their lives will be impenetrable. You will have equipped them with a protective coating that's stronger than the attacks of the stalker.

A print advertisement that always made me laugh comes to mind. A beautiful woodpecker has decided to peck not on a tree but on a wall made of a new synthetic wall-covering material. The wall shows no damage whatsoever, while the woodpecker's beak is accordion pleated. It's a funny picture and tells the story without a word. The point is clear: No one set out to destroy the woodpecker, only to strengthen the target so the woodpecker could do it no harm.

Perhaps you feel inadequate to teach your kids about debt and money management because you've made a mess of your finances. Maybe you really blew it during college and now you're paying for it. Don't let that happen to your kids.

Tell them what happened to you.

Tell them about the people in this book.

Tell them about me, about my boys.

You will never regret the time and effort you put into teaching your kids the basics of good money management.

9

future debtors of america

They're armed and dangerous. The next generation of adults—your kids—wield tremendous economic power but lack financial knowledge. If that's not scary enough, statistics indicate that this generation will make more consumer decisions than any generation before.

Kids are of great importance to the marketing industry, not only because they spend a lot of money themselves but also because of the significant influence they have over what their parents spend on them. The Center for Media Literacy reports that children make up the most lucrative market for many businesses because the youngsters are actually three markets in one:

1. They spend $30 billion a year of their own money on their own desires.[1]

2. They are a future market for most goods and services, a demographic group to be cultivated now.

3. They influence their parents' purchases. Children under the age of twelve influence $100 billion a year in adult spending for things such as groceries, cars, computers, televisions, and where to go on vacation. Parents rely heavily on their kids to be their resident consumer experts.

With children either spending or influencing the spending of billions of dollars each year, marketing techniques have been turned upside down.[2] In the past, the most effective way to sell children's products was through Mom and Dad. Now the opposite is true. Children are the focal point for intense advertising pressure seeking to influence billions of dollars of family spending.[3] Today's teens, the largest group of teenagers ever in American history, also have tremendous economic power. They spend more than $51 billion of their own money each year, and an additional $175 billion is spent on them because they have access to their parents' credit cards. Beyond that they influence the way their families spend another $300 billion a year.[4]

All told, America's kids currently control $1.12 trillion in annual sales of goods and services in this country, according to author and marketing consultant James McNeal, a fact that hasn't escaped the attention of advertisers and marketers. In television commercials aimed at children alone, it is estimated that the industry spends $12 billion per year.[5] There's big money for those who can successfully influence and manipulate the way kids use their economic muscles and spend their money.

They Are Shoppers

Studies show that the average six-year-old goes shopping two to three times a week, visiting at least two kinds of stores, one of which is a grocery store. By age ten, this kid is shopping an average of eleven to twelve times a month, visiting as many as five stores in a single week. That's comparable to the number and variety of shopping trips adults make.

Kids don't go to the store simply to look around. They're there to buy something. If they don't find what they came for, they buy something else. It's not the actual purchase but the act of buying that's important.

The average teen visits a mall fifty-four times a year, compared to thirty-nine times for all other shoppers.[6] Sixty-seven percent of teens and 37 percent of children who have internet access use it to research or buy products online.[7]

Today's teens spend most of their money on themselves, are quite picky, and are very opinionated on what they'll buy. They are brand loyal and more attracted to stores by merchandise than by price. They buy everything imaginable—clothing, fast food, magazines, computers, electronic equipment, music, and entertainment.

Teenage girls—using a powerful combination of allowances, part-time jobs, birthday cash, and easy access to parents' credit cards (one in three high school seniors carries a credit card)—drop an average of eighty-three dollars per week; teenage boys spend eight-four dollars a week.[8]

Advertising

Advertising has become such a part of our culture that we are mostly unaware of the ways it influences our desires and the way we spend our money. Kids are not immune.

How many ads would you imagine invade their little lives? Statistics say that by age seven, children will have seen some 20,000 thirty-second television commercials a year; 360,000 by the time they reach age twenty (and a full 2,000,000 by age sixty-five, just in case you are curious). And that only accounts for television. Just imagine how many other forms of advertising kids see and hear.[9]

Advertisements, "hidden persuaders," have a subtle yet profound influence on the way we think, act, and respond. The goal is to influence us to believe in and then buy specific brands of goods and services. The younger the target, the easier the task.

When asked why the network spent $30 million to create preschool programs, Geraldine Lay Bourne, president of Nickelodeon Children's Television Network, said, "We recognize that if we start getting kids to watch us at this age, we have them for life. That's exactly the reason we're doing it."[10] Bingo.

The combined forces of manufacturers and retailers, both using a variety of advertising media, have tremendous influence over children. In addition to the direct influence advertising has on children, there's a secondary and even more important effect on the parents. If advertisers want to hook a parent, doing so through a child can be very effective.

Babies are exposed to loads of advertising before they can talk, and it's a given in the industry that toddlers recognize company names before their own. Twenty-six percent of children under two have a television in their bedroom.[11]

Just imagine how important that fact is to, say, the McDonald's corporation. The kind of marketing required to turn a commercial symbol such as the golden arches into a national icon, recognizable by every age group, is the result of brilliant marketing. It doesn't just happen.

Because children have such an affinity for computers and things electronic, many marketers are supplementing their outreach to kids through electronic media. To see firsthand the kind of advertising they're using, check out the growing number of kids' sites being established by online services. Dozens of marketers such as McDonald's, Nike, and Coca-Cola have kid-oriented content on the internet. For instance, HappyMeal.com is a children's website with interactive games and activities centered around the famous Happy Meal.

Child-development experts have identified the five key motivators that influence kids: power, freedom, fun, belonging, and mastery. Effective influence peddlers strive to make sure kids experience one or more of these emotions while under the influence of their ads. That element becomes more important in making a sale than the product itself.

There's no way to fully describe or measure the influence being brought to bear on the kids of this country. It's everywhere. The messages vary greatly, but the underlying theme is always there, nagging, compelling them to buy, and assuring them that they deserve to have what they want when they want it.

Television

Television is the number one marketing tool professionals use to reach kids. According to the A. C. Nielsen Co., the average child watches television 1,680 minutes (28 hours) per week.[12]

Included in that group are the heaviest viewers, preschoolers, who watch twenty-six hours a week. Granted, this number becomes somewhat skewed by the fact that much of television time for children involves watching a video rather than commercial programming. Still, much of television advertising targets very young children.

According to TV-Free America, a nonprofit consumer organization, the cumulative effect of nonstop exposure to consumer marketing at an ever earlier age may be profound.[13]

As kids drink in the world around them, many of their cultural encounters—especially on TV—have become little more than sales pitches, devoid of any moral beyond a plea for a purchase. Instead of transmitting a sense of who we are and what we hold important, today's marketing-driven culture is instilling in children the sense that little exists without a sales pitch attached and that self-worth is something you buy at a shopping mall.

"No one ad is bad," says Mary Pipher, clinical psychologist and family life author. "But the combination of four hundred ads a day creates in children a combination of narcissism, entitlement, and dissatisfaction."[14]

Channel One

Channel One is a television news program targeted at teenagers and beamed to school classrooms around the country by satellite that children are required to watch as part of their school day.

Channel One programming is offered to school systems at no cost. The company also donates to the schools all the equipment necessary to receive the program (one satellite dish and two VCRs and TVs per classroom). In return, the school system must require students to view the program every day.

The twelve-minute daily program consists of ten minutes of news and two minutes of commercials. The program reaches nearly six million twelve- to seventeen-year-old students in the country on a daily basis.[15]

On the surface, the Channel One phenomenon appears to be harmless, perhaps even beneficial. After all, one might argue, teens need to know what's going on in the world. Channel One is the way to get it to them in a format they can understand and will accept—and at no cost to the schools.

But Channel One consists of high-tech, fast-paced productions that highlight the commercials rather than the news stories. Their sales literature reads, "Every school day, as many teens watch Channel One as the Super Bowl. Channel One's audience exceeds the combined number of teens watching anything on television during Primetime! Every school day is a Super Bowl! Huge rates. Unsurpassed reach. Unparalleled impact among teen viewers."

Channel One promises to deliver to its big-name corporate advertisers the very hardest-to-reach teen viewers. By terms of the contractual agreements between Channel One and the schools, students must watch the full twelve minutes each day. That means the watching of commercials by this so-called difficult-to-reach teenage audience is mandatory. For this, advertisers such as Nike and Pepsi are willing to pay rates that rival those of the Super Bowl—up to $200,000 for each thirty-second commercial. That alone is a clear indicator of just how commercially successful Channel One is.

To illustrate that success, consider the Skittles story. Channel One consists of news stories and commercials. However, it is often difficult to distinguish between the two. Producers purposely blur the line between commercials and the news.

Some years ago, a Channel One series of ads for Skittles candy began with what appeared to be a newscaster introducing another news segment. He begins the story when a snowstorm of static suddenly interrupts. As Monty Python-esque images fill the screen, a voice-over says, "We interrupt this class for a temporary fun emergency—for the next thirty seconds think only fun thoughts." A succession of "fun thoughts" follows.[16]

A series of five "fun emergencies" was so successful in boosting sales of Skittles that the company booked ten more spots of the same format for the following season.

Clearly, Channel One has found success in influencing and manipulating the buying habits of a huge segment of this nation's teens, those hard-to-reach "light" television viewers. In a society in which television ratings are life or death, Channel One doesn't have to worry. Their audiences can't take a bathroom break or click through the commercials. Channel One can count on a captive audience five days a week, month after month after month.

How serious is this influence? At the very least, I have no doubt that regular viewing of Channel One reinforces materialistic attitudes. Just what we don't need.

They Are Uninformed

If I've learned anything from the stacks of mail I've received over the years, it's that America's kids are leaving home without knowing about money, credit, and debt. They're not learning it at school or at home.

Do a Google search of "kids and money" and you'll get millions of hits for everything from gadgets to games and myriad sites aimed at educating youth on things financial. Great. If there's one thing the next generation of adults will need to know, it's how to save and stay out of debt. Unfortunately, all that effort isn't paying off very well. In 2010, the average high school senior flunked, with a score of 48 percent, the annual Jump$tart Coalition for Personal Financial Literacy test, which measures how prepared these young adults are to make critical purchasing decisions once they graduate from high school. In 1997, the average score on the very same test was 57 percent. The same test given to adults produced curious results. The adults scored only sixteen points higher than the students. Employing even the most liberal scoring procedures, the results are indisputable. Everyone flunked.

Four-year college students took a similar test in their junior and senior years. While the scores were considerably higher than those of the high schoolers tested, they didn't come close to passing either.

If all of this financial ignorance isn't bad enough, consider this worrisome fact: Students are financially ignorant but don't know it—and worse, don't care.

Here's a snippet of recent results of the 2008 Survey of Financial Literacy among High School Students,[17] which is routinely given to students nationwide.

- Only 28 percent could precisely define buying on credit.
- Only 28 percent could precisely define a mortgage.
- Only 25 percent could precisely define a budget.
- Only 7 percent could precisely define life insurance.
- Only 4 percent could reasonably define Social Security.
- Only 5 percent could precisely define compound interest.
- Only 3 percent could precisely define mutual funds.
- Eighty-eight percent of those surveyed said they are either very good or pretty good at managing their money.
- Thirty percent said they are not at all interested in financial information or money matters.
- Only 13 percent said they are very interested in such topics.

Cause for concern? You'd better believe it. The most strik-ing finding in the test of high schoolers is how little seniors know about the products and services they will encounter after graduation—items such as credit, checking and savings accounts, and auto insurance.

By the time college students reach their junior year, they have already bought banking and insurance products, rented some type of living quarters, accepted credit cards, and pur-chased items on credit. And they've likely made considerable mistakes in doing so—mistakes that will have an impact on their futures.

Our youngsters are heading for adulthood unequipped to handle the temptation of easy credit. They are prone to excessive consumerism but lack the financial intelligence they will need to effectively use the economic power they have. It is this power and ignorance, combined with material desires, that makes kids easy marks for the world of commercial influence and consumer credit.

10

the trouble with debt

though I find the chore distasteful, I must show you the dark side of consumer debt. The world gives this type of credit living a glamorous spin. It says an approved credit application is a badge of honor, tangible evidence that you are worthy to enter a superior level of consumerism.

I am seriously opinionated about consumer debt. My opinions are anything but positive. For that I do not apologize. Furthermore, I intend to do everything I can to convince you that consumer debt is hazardous to your children's futures.

Debt-proofing kids requires parents to pass on values to their children. You cannot pass on values you do not possess. For your children to achieve financial confidence at the level that will hold them in good stead in a world of economic turmoil, they must believe with all their hearts that consumer debt is wrong and should not enter their lives. But first you must believe. So while I do care about you, I confess my first concern is for your kids.

And now you know—I have a hidden agenda. I'm using you to get to your kids. Clever, huh?

I didn't learn about debt in a university lecture hall. My classroom has been my life and the lives of thousands of people I've met over the past twenty years. I know consumer debt—which is light-years from just knowing about it. Because of my intimate relationship with it, I absolutely despise consumer debt.

Two Kinds of Debt

Like fireworks, debt comes in two varieties—safe and highly explosive.

Secured debt, like the "safe and sane" fireworks we set off on Independence Day, carries a certain amount of risk. However, if you follow the instructions using ordinary precaution, everything will be just fine.

Unsecured debt (also called consumer debt) is like high-risk, explosive fireworks. Under all circumstances it is extremely dangerous. It promises a spectacular experience and delivers an initial burst of glory. But sooner or later those who think they can play without getting burned wake up with nothing to show for the experience except severe injuries and a pile of ashes.

The CARD Act of 2009, which became effective in February 2009, made changes to the law, some of which were good for consumers who carry debt. It outlawed a few unfair practices of the credit-card companies and banks having to do with the ways they charge penalties and fees. The changes were fine, but in the end they only caused the issuers to find new ways to recoup their losses. One way was to increase interest rates and minimum payments. For people who were already carrying heavy loads of unsecured credit-card debt, these changes did not help. If you find yourself in that position, you are possibly nodding your head in agreement, fully aware of just how injurious unsecured credit-card debt can be. I will go so far as to say that it is toxic.

Secured Debt

When a lender holds an asset that has a monetary value equal to the amount of the loan, that loan is considered to be secured. The asset acts as the lender's guarantee that the borrower will repay the loan.

The asset is called collateral. If the borrower defaults on the loan, the lender takes the collateral as payment for the loan. The collateral is a "safety valve" to protect both the borrower and the lender. Secured debts are safe debts. Real estate and automobiles are the most common forms of collateral.

Secured debts don't carry a high potential of harm because (1) the borrower goes through a qualifying process; (2) the protective nature of the collateral provides a way of escape; and (3) interest rates are typically lower on secured loans.

While it is always better not to borrow, we live in a time when it would be impossible for most people to buy a home or an automobile without a secured loan. These are circumstances under which secured debt is appropriate.

113

Unsecured Debt

Consumer, or unsecured debt, is an uncollateralized loan. There is no security. The borrower exchanges a signature and a promise for the lender's dough. The most common types of consumer debt are credit-card balances, personal loans, installment loans, student loans, and other unsecured obligations, such as dental and medical bills.

If the borrower defaults for any reason, the lender has the right under the law to come after the borrower, his credit report, and anything else he can get his hands on. Unsecured debts are extremely hazardous because (1) there is no qualifying process to make sure the borrower isn't in over his head; (2) there is no "safety valve" to protect the parties if things don't go as planned; and (3) interest rates on consumer debt are outrageously high.

Debt makes an arrogant presumption on the future. Let's say you have your eye on a new computer that costs $1,500. You are strapped for cash but have your heart set on it, and the store will gladly finance the purchase. You "buy" it for $1,500 at 18 percent interest with monthly payments equal to 3 percent of the outstanding balance. It will take twelve years and three months to pay for the computer. Including $1,298 in interest, the real cost of the computer is $2,798.

Beyond the store's refund policy, there is no backing out on this debt. It is unsecured. You owe the money plus interest no matter what. If you get sick and can't work, you still owe the money. If the computer dies, even if it is stolen, you still owe the money.

Who can predict what will happen in your life over the next twelve years and three months? Will the creditor make allowances for things such as unemployment? Don't count on it. You will owe the money no matter what. The creditor will show no mercy.

When you bought the computer, you paid for it with credit because you were strapped for cash. Why will things be any different next month? How do you know you'll even have a job, let alone an extra $45 to make the first payment and all the others right through number 147?

Do you see the arrogance in this transaction? By agreeing to pay back $2,798 with absolutely no way to escape, you make a statement that you can foresee the future. You promise to pay this debt based on an assumption that you will have your health and the abilities you take for granted.

And then there's the little matter of obsolescence. The chances of this computer being anything but a dinosaur in twelve years and three months are slim to none. This country is full of people who are paying for things they don't have anymore with money they don't yet have—and no real assurance they'll ever get it.

The Trouble with Debt

Debt enslaves. Even though written thousands of years ago, King Solomon's wise words are as timely as if they were torn from today's headlines: "The poor are ruled by the rich, and those who borrow are slaves of moneylenders" (Prov. 22:7).

Slavery is a despicable circumstance. Any loss of personal freedom is degrading and depressing. When you take on unsecured debt, that's exactly what you choose—a form of slavery. Your creditors "own" you as long as you owe them money. Their grip is unrelenting. They are legally entitled to their portion of your paycheck, and you dare not forget that. There are stiff punishments for "slaves" who don't perform for their masters as promised.

The most curious thing about the slave-master relationship is how some debtors, miserable as they are, keep adding to their debt load, extending their sentence of servitude with every new purchase.

Debt advances dissatisfaction. Consumer credit enables impulsive spending. Shopping with plastic, the cardholder can make impulsive decisions and purchases. Consumer credit enables instant gratification. When things come too easily, we don't appreciate them. We make silly decisions, impulsive purchases that quickly lose their appeal, leaving us completely unsatisfied with a house full of stuff, a pile of debt, and a raging case of affluenza (an extreme form of materialism in which consumers overwork and accumulate high levels of debt to purchase more goods). The things we thought would satisfy choke the joy right out of our lives.

Debt destroys options. When burdened with debt, you give up the option to quit a job to return to school or to leave a miserable job to take one that pays less but would allow you to do something you truly love. Debt prevents you from following your dreams or your heart's desire to be of service in some profound way. Each time you increase your debt, you eliminate another option.

Debt destroys relationships. A young man wrote to me recently. It seems the love of his life broke off their engagement because she couldn't see herself starting out married life $23,000 in the hole due to his reckless spending. There was little I could do but encourage him to get out of the hole and not make debt a pattern of his life. I also told him she did him a big favor. That kind of wake-up call early in life was a gift for which he should send her a thank-you note.

Debt is an equal opportunity misery. Never before in the history of this country has credit been so available and debt so attractive. A bank credit card is available to most anyone who has two things: an ID and a pulse.

The average person views an approved credit application as a badge of honor, a sign he has arrived, the concrete proof he is certainly able to handle this amount of debt. Nothing could be further from the truth.

Credit-card issuers see you as a risk worth taking to increase their profit margins. They don't care if you are income challenged or have other pressing obligations. It's not their concern if you get in over your head. They're banking on the fact that you'll accept a substantial amount of debt, habitually pay only the minimum monthly payment, and never be able to pay the balance in full. Fitting into that profile and operating according to their highest expectations make you nothing more than a pawn on their chessboard of high finance. Debt does not discriminate. It offers misery to all.

Debt is hazardous to your wealth. Remember that computer deal we dissected a few pages back? You know, the $1,500 computer that ends up costing $2,798 after twelve years but has a functional life of five (and that may be too generous these days). With interest, the price is almost double the actual price tag.

Now apply that principle to everything bought on credit. People with huge consumer debt have to make twice as much to live half as well as families or individuals who live debt-free. Because their debt obligations are so steep, debtors don't believe they have enough money to give to charity or to save for the future.

Debt is a terrible thief.

11

tear down attitudes of entitlement

It is strangely ironic that the freedoms and affluence we enjoy in our society are the very things that stand to ruin our children if not addressed early and effectively.

You will recall from chapter 1 that the consumer-credit industry is doing all it can to get your kids to fall for the buy-now, pay-later lifestyle. If you do nothing to intervene, statistics indicate that your child is headed for a life that will be severely impacted not by credit—credit is not the problem here—but by the debt it can create.

When the following three characteristics occur at the same time in the heart and mind of a child, they create a kind of "perfect storm" that has all the likelihood of creating a disastrous situation:

1. attitudes of entitlement
2. financial ignorance
3. glamour of easy spending

The antidotes for this lethal combination are the subjects of this chapter and chapters 12 and 13.

For our debt-proofing purposes, "entitlement" is that demanding attitude that says, "I deserve it now even if I haven't earned it or cannot pay for it." Some call it the gimmes, others the I-wants. No matter what you call it, this attitude is running rampant, and not only among kids. Entitlement affects kids and adults alike.

Entitlement is subtle. It creeps into our lives when we compare our lifestyles and possessions to those of the people we respect and want to be like. It shows up in new parents who throw all caution to the wind when it comes to nursery furnishings and "mandatory" equipment. It shows up in two-income families who, because they work so hard, feel they deserve to have nice things. It shows up in adults who feel compelled to conform to society's relentless ratcheting up of standards.

The eighteenth-century French philosopher Denis Diderot wrote an essay entitled "Regrets on Parting with My Old Dressing Gown." It seems someone gave Diderot an exquisite gift—a scarlet dressing gown (not something your typical guy today would get too excited about, but remember this was in the 1700s). Diderot was so happy to get a new dressing gown that he promptly threw his old one away. Curiously, he hadn't noticed how tattered the old gown was because it was comfortable and blended into his surroundings.

The contrast between the new scarlet gown and everything else in his study was startling. While Diderot was wearing the gown, he couldn't stop noticing the threadbare tapestries, the worn chair, and the beat-up bookcases. Piece by piece he replaced everything with something more closely suited to the elegance of his robe. Diderot closes his essay regretting ever receiving the scarlet robe that forced everything else into conformity. Today, marketing professionals and consumer researchers call this constant reach for conformity the "Diderot effect."

Entitlement is the standard message of marketing and advertising. Look carefully at everything that shows up in your mailbox this week. All the marketing or advertising pieces carry some underlying message that you deserve this, you need that, and you'll never be completely satisfied until you do this or go there. Clothing catalogs point out changes in fashion; linen stores introduce the latest seasonal colors. The message to keep up is relentless. The push for conformity creates attitudes of dissatisfaction and entitlement.

With the explosion in the availability of consumer credit, which has encouraged conspicuous consumption, attitudes of entitlement have become all too standard. At every turn it seems something or someone is fanning the flames of entitlement in our lives—and our children's lives too.

Attitudes of entitlement, both yours and your children's, are an enemy that, if not dealt with, will surely sabotage your efforts to develop financial confidence in your kids.

Live an Understated Lifestyle

A frugal lifestyle, where you live below your means, is the best environment in which to raise kids. When children observe their parents consuming carefully, making wise spending decisions, choosing not to buy the biggest and the best, and not living on credit, they begin to assimilate those values.

Rather than always telling your kids, "We can't afford that," a better response is, "We don't choose to spend our money in that way." This sends the message that even though you may be able to afford to buy what your kids want, too much consumption is not good. Telling your kids you cannot afford this or that or to go here or there tells them only one thing: We are poor. If we weren't so poor, we could have this or that and go here or there. That sends the message that money is the key to happiness—if we just had enough money, we could be perfectly happy.

Kids worry about being poor, and if you just leave it at "We can't afford it," you run the risk of sending them the wrong message or causing them to worry about things children ought not to worry about.

By telling your children, "We don't choose to spend our money on that," you send a positive message that you have money but make intelligent choices about how to spend it.

Don't aspire to look like the most affluent family in the neighborhood by living as if you have a big bank balance. If yours is a one-earner family, don't live the lifestyle of your two-paycheck friends. Rather than constantly striving to keep up, look for ways to downshift. Don't live to consume and don't base your self-worth on your net worth.

Discover the Real Need

Attitudes of entitlement are often a symptom. There are times parents get so caught up in the frantic pace of the daily grind that they don't realize that most of what children need cannot be bought. Children need time and attention, conversation with their parents, and guidance. They need to know they are significant and valuable and that someone is interested in their moral development. Maybe it's not the new outfit or the electronic device that's the real issue after all.

Become a Giving Family

The best antidote for attitudes of entitlement is to give away the very thing you crave. Giving takes our eyes off ourselves and our insatiable desires. It works in children as well. Get your kids involved in supporting your church's outreach ministries and community food pantries. Give to a missionary family that has children of similar ages to yours. "Adopt" an orphan in a third-world country. There are so many ways your family can become intentional givers. Giving takes effort and requires commitment, but the benefits both in personal and spiritual growth and in tearing down attitudes of entitlement will be invaluable.

Limit Shopping

Stay away from malls and throw mail-order catalogs in the recycle bin the minute they show up. As much as possible, do your necessary shopping solo—without kids. Overexposing children to the grocery store, the mall, or the warehouse club inevitably creates desire.

Let the shopping trips that include the children be for a specific purpose, not simply to wander around to see what kind of desire you can create.

When the kids are with you in a store, make sure you follow the debt-proof rules:

- Shop with a list.
- Shop with cash.
- Find what you've come to buy.
- Leave.

Limit Television Viewing

Monitor children's television viewing. For very young children, select noncommercial viewing. Find a way to let the kids help limit their TV time.

Here's an idea. Let the kids decorate popsicle sticks or tongue depressors. Use them to keep track of earned television viewing time. One stick equals thirty minutes of TV time. Devise a plan for the kids to earn sticks by reading books, picking up toys, etc. Make a rule: no sticks, no TV.

Talk with your kids about commercial advertisements and the real message. Teach them to see through messages that suggest if you drink a certain soft drink or buy a certain brand of makeup you'll be like the celebrity in the ad.

Teach your kids to play the game "What's the Value?" (could also be called "What's the Lie?"). After each commercial,

ask them what value the ad was trying to sell. Was it pleasure, possessions, or prestige (prestige could also be power
or popularity)? The first person to answer correctly wins.
She gets bonus points if she can explain the reasoning behind
the response.

Commercial advertisements create false needs in all of us,
but particularly in children. Children are literal in their thinking. Begin looking at this commercialized world through your
children's very literal eyes and ways of thinking. You'll find
yourself "believing" all kinds of lies.

If you have children in schools that carry Channel One,
rather than forbidding them to participate, prepare them.
Have them write down and then report to you the commercials they see each day along with their assessment of the
lies the commericals were trying to tell. Were they pleasure,
possessions, or prestige? If you have any influence in the
school, suggest that "What's the Value?" might be an excellent follow-up to the daily presentation in class. Everything
you do to get your children thinking and making their own
evaluations about what the world is trying to make them
believe will hasten the day they are debt-proofed.

Consider TV-free periods. Start with a day; go to a full
week. It's an enlightening experience.

Find Alternatives

Your goal in tearing down attitudes of entitlement is to
direct your children's attention and desires away from the

commercialization of their lives. Spending less time at the mall and more time in wholesome venues will support that goal.

Create a desire in your children to go to the library. Capitalize on the fact that most libraries allow us to borrow books, videos, etc., rather than having to buy them. Push the community aspect of sharing and supporting literature. Attend the special presentations. If your library has a membership fee (many do these days), gladly purchase a membership and then use it.

Trade mall time for park time. Make it a point to visit all the parks in your city. Find the hiking trails and bike paths. Call the local Chamber of Commerce to find the factories or manufacturing plants in your area that conduct tours. Make a list of all the places you can be tourists in your own town.

Maintain Financial Privacy

Parents should never tell their children how much money they earn. Whether you are at the poverty level or well-heeled, your children should not be privy to your annual income. Kids don't need that information. When they have it, they don't know how to interpret it.

One woman shared with me how as a child her entire attitude about life and material things changed the day she learned her father made a six-figure income. Everything shifted when she decided they were the richest people in the world and she deserved whatever she wanted.

If your child asks how much you earn, answer back with the question, "Why do you want to know?" If the child worries you'll be homeless tomorrow, assure her that is not the case. If your child asks so he can brag to his friends about how rich he is, the answer should be something like, "That is Mommy and Daddy's private information." It is okay for parents to have financial privacy.

Take a Kid's View of Plastic

Credit cards, debit cards, and ATM cards are stand-ins for money—they are not the real thing. They confuse the issue of who's paying for what.

It's important that you make money real for your kids and that they observe you living in that reality as well. Parents should live a cash lifestyle in front of their children. Kids shouldn't see your plastic. They shouldn't see you use it, and they shouldn't see it in your wallet.

Children are very literal. This is what children see when you pay for goods or services with a credit or debit card. Someone swipes the card through the machine, the little clicking sounds commence, you sign your name, and then you get the card back, plus the merchandise too. What the child sees is that you got something for nothing because you have a plastic magic key. It does not matter to him if you pay the entire bill in full every month or that your debit card is actually taking money directly from your checking account. Kids cannot process abstract thoughts.

Even your older children don't need to see you living contrary to the values you are teaching them. The constant use of plastic desensitizes children to the harsh realities of debt-filled living. Remember, debt-proofed kids live a cash lifestyle. Seeing their parents live that way validates those family values.

What about ATM transactions? Kids see you put a piece of plastic in the wall (remember, credit, debit, and ATM cards all look alike), and what happens? Clicking sounds and you get back the card and free money! It didn't cost you anything. All you need is a plastic key.

ATM cards, credit cards, debit cards, and checkbooks should be used, if at all, out of the presence of kids. When kids are around, it should be cash only.

Rethink Christmas

There's nothing like the Christmas holiday to encourage entitlement fever in all of us. But there are lots of things you can do to keep this holiday in line with your new understated lifestyle.

First, make the season a time of giving and sharing. It's a perfect time of the year to help your kids go through their toys and clothes to scale back and downsize in anticipation of some new stuff. Let the kids go with you to deliver items to a shelter or to a needy organization. At this time of year, your time is most valuable; give that precious gift to your kids. Spend time, make memories, have fun.

Impose reasonable limits on the length of wish lists. Don't enable unreasonable longing and yearning by the presence of catalogs and toy store magazines in your home. Help your kids make gifts.

Measure carefully every activity so that it fits into a larger picture of making this a time we give more than we receive. Point to the symbolism of giving and the real reason we celebrate.

Educate Grandparents and Other Benefactors

I had another life-changing experience on July 7, 2009, when our first grandson, Elijah, came into the world. I used to worry that my natural propensity to overshop, overindulge, and overdo might surely gurgle to the surface if we were ever blessed with grandchildren. I was right. However, I am happy to report that so far I have learned from past mistakes and I'm holding strong. We are finding ways to bless our sweet little Eli's life without ruining him or ticking off his parents.

Grandparents often sabotage good work that has gone on between parents and their children by feeling they must always be gifting the grandchildren. If you give too much and too often, you interfere with the principles and values the family is establishing.

Bob and Dot, who have several grandchildren and hope to have more, have hit upon what appears to be a great plan. Upon the birth of each grandchild, they open a mutual fund custodial account for the baby's education. Then for each birthday, they give one nice outfit, one special toy, and a deposit into the investment account.

At Christmas, each grandchild receives one nice outfit, one special toy, and a gift certificate to a professional photographer. I love their program because it's something the parents can plan on (especially those regular trips to the photographer), it's not overindulgent, and it frees Bob and Dot during the rest of the year to just have fun with their grandchildren without the kids always expecting a gift.

Rethink Birthdays

A child's birthday should be the best day of the whole year. Set a spending limit ahead of time and keep to the cash-only rule.

Think of ways to make the child feel special that don't involve gifts and lots of money. Decorate his room with balloons. Make it a no-chores day. Treat her like a princess for a full twenty-four hours.

If you have a traditional party, keep a lid on the quantity of gifts as much as possible. I know of families who designate certain birthdays the big milestones (five, ten, sixteen, eighteen), having parties those years and opting for family celebrations in the years in between.

But of all the times that you want to convey to your children how wonderful they are and how thankful you are for them, it's on their birthdays. You can do that without spending a great deal of money.

Use the Debt-Proof Plan

By far the best antidote for attitudes of entitlement is to put your children on the debt-proof plan of this book. Going "on salary" at about age ten will put the brakes on attitudes of entitlement as your child begins to control his or her own desires and perspectives, from the inside out.

Clearly, attitudes of entitlement are a serious problem. But they are not terminal. Diligent parents who are willing to be consistent examples and limit setters will find success in tearing down attitudes that have the potential to do great harm.

12

develop financial intelligence

It takes relatively little effort to teach kids about money. And the payoff is enormous. If you are diligent to work this teaching into the normal course of family life, it will come as naturally as teaching kids good manners or how to do laundry. It will be as ordinary as teaching them how to mow the lawn or wash the car.

This chapter contains basic money facts your children need to know, along with ideas and suggestions for how you can present them in a kid-friendly way. Not a one-time lesson, this information will be best taught as it is lived out in your home.

Money Management

At the foundation of your children's financial intelligence should be this undeniable truth: It is not the amount of money you have but what you do with it that matters. This is true for a child managing a five-dollar-a-week allowance or a corporate executive with a five-thousand-dollar-a-week salary.

For many years of my life, I didn't know this truth. On the contrary, I believed that more money was the answer. I was convinced that if we just made more money, won the lottery, or received some unexpected inheritance, all of our money problems would vanish. But the more we made, the worse our problems became. Because I didn't know how to manage what we had, more was never enough. We didn't save, we didn't give, we didn't plan, and we had no idea where all the money went.

Unless your children learn simple, wise money management techniques, more money will never be enough.

Teaching Kids about Money Management

A great way to teach this basic financial truth is through storytelling. Here are a few of my favorites, true stories you can tell your kids.

Neil McCarthy, who started saving money when he was very young, began investing in the stock market when he was thirty-four, in the 1970s. Today he has a net worth of about $2.1 million. When stocks went down, he bought more. He contributed the maximum to both his IRA and his 401(k), and his employer matched 100 percent. That's truly free money—no risk. The big payoff came during the 1990s bull market when his stock doubled in three or four years, suddenly reaching $1 million. His number one piece of advice that made all the difference is this: "If you wait to save out of what's left over from your salary, it's not going to happen. Pay yourself first."[1]

Petro "Pete" Kulynych started at the bottom as the bookkeeper for a small hardware store in North Carolina, earning twenty-five dollars a week. But he never looked at the twenty-five dollars as the amount he had to spend. He would always ask himself, "How much of this can I *not* spend so I have more to save?" That store became the first in the Lowe's hardware chain, and Mr. Kulynych ended up a top executive.[2]

Mike Domek started his business with $100 in 1992. He had run out of money for college and decided to try ticket brokering full-time to save up for school. He launched TicketsNow, an online company, seven years later. Domek's projected sales for 2005 were $120 million. In 2008, TicketMaster bought the company for $265 million.[3]

Share with your kids stories you read and hear about people who, like those above, illustrate the principle of money management. Negative examples are also effective. Watch for stories of people who win the lottery, live like a king, and in no time at all file for bankruptcy because they just didn't know how to manage money. Stories like that are amazingly common.

Use the jar system. It's simple, it's cheap, and it works really well. Take clear glass or plastic jars and label them "Needs," "Long-term savings," "Short-term savings," "Giving," "Spending," and so on. Even preschoolers understand the jar system. Teach your kids how to split their money according to your family's basic money management rules.

What Kids Need to Know about Managing Money

1. It's not how much money you make but how you manage what you have that matters.
2. You don't need a lot of money to be a good money manager. A small amount of money well managed is far more important than a lot of money wasted.
3. In the same way you have life rules, you need money rules that guide the way you handle your money.

Giving

It's a universal principle, a simple concept: Give back part of everything you receive. Giving away some of the money that flows into our lives exposes our lives and our finances to something supernatural. Teach your kids always to give back a percentage of their income before they save or spend.

This giving principle is really simple to teach to young kids. They don't question; they don't try to reason. They will simply believe you when you teach them that spending all of your money is a selfish thing to do.

Because kids are anxious to please, they respond well to the idea that it is important to show we're thankful and to help others. It is a good habit to become a giver.

Teaching Kids about Giving

Brainstorm with your child about good reasons to give. It helps people who are less fortunate or who are sick. It helps volunteers and people who are giving their lives to fulfill an important mission. It helps you focus on the needs of others.

Giving money helps you become a responsible person. When people think only of themselves, they become selfish and self-centered. Giving makes the world a nicer place to live. Think about this: If everybody became a giver, there would be fewer hungry kids.

If you are part of a church, you may want to teach your children to give there. There are also other places you can give in your community such as homeless shelters or rescue missions. Together with your child, make a list of ten organizations to which your child may give money. Help your child learn more about each organization and decide on one or more to which to contribute.

Once you think like a giver, you will keep your ears open for special needs.

What Kids Need to Know about Giving

1. Giving always comes first, before saving or spending.
2. Giving 10 percent is a reasonable amount.
3. There are many places and ways to give. You can watch your money help in many kinds of circumstances.

Saving

Saving money means choosing to keep it in a safe place instead of spending it. No matter how small the amount of money your kids receive, saving part of it should be a given. Saving money will become a lifelong habit in no time at all if it is approached as mandatory to right living. There are several kinds of savings that your kids need to learn about.

Teaching Kids about Saving

Long-term savings. Think of this as serious savings—money you don't touch, borrow, or spend. Adults call it retirement savings; kids don't need to call their long-term savings anything specific. It's the act of always saving for the long term that is important.

Long-term savings should be kept in a safe, interest-bearing account and left to grow. Some banks and credit unions still offer simple school savings accounts in which minimums and fees are waived. Teaching kids from a young age to pay themselves before they spend will help this become a habit when they are grown.

Once a significant amount has been saved, consider moving long-term savings into a more aggressive vehicle such as a mutual fund account in which the child is the account owner and the parent is the custodian.

Short-term savings. This is the way you teach your kids to accumulate enough money to buy something that costs more than they have on a weekly or monthly basis, such as a bike, new doll, or video game.

Short-term saving teaches the joy of delayed gratification and the value of truly yearning for something. "Save first, spend later" is a motto your kids won't learn at the mall or from television but a sound principle they need to learn from you.

Because kids are so literal, providing some kind of visual aid will help them see and understand the principle of saving to buy things that cost more than they receive in a week or a month. Collecting the money in a jar is a good idea. Other visuals work well too.

Find a picture that represents the item he wants. Maybe it's a bike or a special toy. Make a chart and attach the picture to the top. Calculate the full price of the item including tax. Divide this by the amount the child elects to put into short-term savings to determine how many saving periods will be required.

Mark off large squares below the picture representing the periods it will take to save the money he'll need. Inside each square write the amount to be saved. Attach an envelope to the poster. Each time your child receives his income, he can place the stipulated savings amount in the envelope and mark off a square. Each time a savings deposit is made into the envelope and a square is marked off, he sees himself moving closer to the goal.

Saving money consistently is like riding a bike or learning to type. At first the activity is awkward and a little shaky. It may not feel right. But through consistent practice—repeating the same action over and over again—the activity will become automatic.

If your children develop the habit of always paying themselves (after they've given some away) before they spend or pay others, saving will be as much a part of their lives as anything else you teach them to do on a regular basis.

What Kids Need to Know about Saving

1. If you always save some of your money—before you even think about spending—you will never be broke.

2. Long-term savings (money you leave alone so it can earn interest over a long period of time) is mandatory. It's the right way to manage money.

3. Short-term savings (money you accumulate for something you want) is optional but a great way to learn delayed gratification.

4. Saving money can be as gratifying as spending money. The difference? The good feeling you get from saving goes on and on, while the fun of spending doesn't last very long.

Needs and Wants

Is something a necessity or a luxury? Essential or optional? We live in a culture in which the lines between needs and wants have become terribly blurred.

Spending is probably the first financial concept your kids will understand. Even toddlers have an uncanny ability to make the connection between money and candy or toys. Giving, saving, and investing, however, have to be taught, as does distinguishing between different types of spending. That's where the necessity for teaching the difference between needs and wants comes in.

Needs are necessities, things we must have to live—things such as shelter, clothes, food, and medicine. Wants are things we like that make our lives fun and enjoyable. It is not wrong to want things. Sometimes it is good to want things that make our lives easier or more enjoyable. However, kids must learn that needs come first and that even adults cannot have everything they want.

Teaching Kids the Difference between Needs and Wants

It takes practice to tell the difference between a need and a want. You can play informal games with your kids during a meal, in the car, or at other times to help them learn. Let television commercials, print ads, or billboards be your game material.

Have the kids determine if the product advertised is a need or a want. The first one with the right answer—and explanation—wins that round. You should expect some lively conversations, especially with your older kids or teens.

For example, you see an advertisement for Nike tennis shoes. Are they a need or a want? Well, shoes are a need, but the Nike brand name is a want—often a very expensive upgrade. That observation could easily lead to a conversation about brand loyalty and why customers feel pressured to spend twice the price just to get a certain brand. Do they think they will be like the celebrity who endorses that brand? Is it emotional appeal? Belief in misleading claims?

Or have your children answer this question: What if I could have everything I want? Have them make a list of all the things they would have if they could have everything they want. Next, they need to answer questions such as, Where would I keep everything I want? How would I make sure my things were safe and secure? How would I enjoy all of these things? It doesn't take long for children to understand that having everything they think they want can ruin their lives.

What Kids Need to Know about Needs and Wants

1. Needs are essential; wants are optional.
2. It is not wrong to want things. Just remember that your wants will always exceed your means.
3. A true need is never realized while you are in a store. If you really needed it, you knew that before you left home.

Spending Record

A spending record is a tracking device. It shows where your money goes. Teaching your kids to keep a written record of where their money goes is a habit that will help them in the future. Tracking expenses in a written format demands focus and keeps spending on a more intelligent level. A written spending record has the effect of plugging up money leaks. It teaches kids to balance income and expenses, a skill that will come in handy once they are on their own. Start them young and the process will become a lifelong habit.

Teaching Kids about a Spending Record

While it would not be advisable to expect a spending record from a preschooler, an older child can easily keep a log of where his money goes. Some parents go so far as to "replace" only the amount of money the child can account for in writing. For example, a child receiving a fifty-dollar-a-month salary would have to produce a spending record that accounts for all of that amount (including saving and giving) in order to receive the next month's salary. That is a severe measure but can be quite effective.

Teach your children that "to whom much is given, much is required." When we receive money, we must be responsible with it. Keeping a record of where our money goes is the way we become good money managers. A spending record keeps money from leaking out of our lives.

Get a notebook. Use this notebook as a spending record for your child. Show your child how to write down all expenditures, i.e., $10 for long-term savings; $10 for church offering; $2 for short-term savings; $6 for a movie ticket, etc. The goal is that the spending record will balance with his or her income.

After a few months, your child will be ready to move on to the spending plan. All of the data gleaned from the spending record (where the money went) can be used to make a written plan of where it will go next month.

What Kids Need to Know about a Spending Record

1. It is important to keep track of where your money goes. Write it down.
2. During the month, compare your spending record with your income. It won't take long for you to make them balance. For instance, if you get ten dollars a week as allowance or salary, your spending record at the end of the week should add up to ten dollars, because you will have written down every cent you gave away, saved, and spent.

3. A spending record is the way to make sure money doesn't leak out of your life without your approval.

Spending Plan

Some people call it a budget. Personally, that word gives me a rash, so I prefer the term *spending plan*. Your kids will too.

A written spending plan is simply the easiest way to match income to expenses. A spending plan is like a road map. It shows you where you are, where you need to go, and how to get there. Even a young child can learn to write down how she plans to spend her money.

Teaching Kids about a Spending Plan

To help your child understand the need for a written plan, use the example of building a house. It would be foolish for a contractor to go to the lumberyard, buy a truckload of wood, dump it on an empty lot, and just start building. No builder in his right mind would set out to do something important like building a house without a plan. It's called a blueprint.

A spending plan is simply a blueprint that helps you build your financial life. Kids can understand the need for making a plan when something is really important. When you plan ahead of time how you will spend your money, you have control over it. You make the decisions. If you don't make a plan and spend money on any old thing without much thought, you lose control. It's not critical at first, but if you start a pattern of losing control, after a while your money will control you.

To make a spending plan, gather information from a past spending record or two. Using this information, help your child plan how he will spend his money the next month. Use the plan to decrease spending, increase short-term savings, or add an additional short-term savings goal.

What Kids Need to Know about a Spending Plan

1. You should always make a written plan for how you intend to spend your money. Your spending plan should include your plans for giving and saving.

2. A plan that is not written down is only a dream. You might think you can remember your plan in your head, but it's always better to write it down.

3. You can make a weekly spending plan or a monthly plan—whatever works best for you. Keep it in a special place where you can refer to it often.

4. Every month when you make a new spending plan, adjust it according to what happened last month. Example: If you planned to spend $5 on a ticket to the movies but ended up spending $7.50 because you bought a snack, remember what happened if you plan to go to the movies again. Make that adjustment so your plan and your actual spending match.

Banking

Saving money is very habit-forming, so the earlier your child begins to save, the better. Learning the wonders of how a real bank works is going to get that saving habit rooted in his or her young life. Your kids will enjoy watching their balance grow.

Teaching Kids about Banking

Teaching your older children the concept of banking can be done in a variety of ways. If you live close to a bank, take your child in to meet a teller and learn about deposits and endorsing checks. Younger children, however, might respond more favorably to a family banking system as a precursor to the traditional institution.

The Bank of Mom and Dad might work like this. Set up a system complete with checkbooks and deposit slips. Let the kids deposit their allowances with you and write checks against the Bank of M&D when they want to give or spend their money. Show kids how to keep a check register (this doesn't preclude the need for a spending record) and keep a running balance of what's in their account. The banker's job, of course, is either to pay the check or bounce it if there are insufficient funds.

One father I heard from set up the Bank of Dad. His generous interest-bearing accounts taught even his five-year-old the joy of watching his money grow. His rule was that money left in the family bank for more than one week began earning interest.

Another family followed the traditional Jamaican custom called "su-su." In essence, a family forms a partnership, with each member agreeing to deposit a specific amount at a specific time each month. Then, each month the entire bank goes to one member of the family partnership with everyone taking a turn. By the end of a full cycle, each family member has had the joy of receiving one large sum of money. No interest is involved, but this does eliminate the element of risk and teaches kids that consistent saving results in great benefit.

Older kids and teens should learn the fundamentals of reconciling a checking account. If you are not in the habit of doing this yourself, start. If you have a computer, you might consider simple accounting software that allows you to track and reconcile your checking account electronically. Your kids will pick this up quickly!

Whatever method you use, it is important to teach the concept of traditional banks, including checking and savings accounts, to your kids early enough that they feel comfortable with it by the time they leave home.

What Kids Need to Know about Banking

1. There are two kinds of bank accounts: savings accounts that pay you interest and checking accounts that allow you to spend at will.
2. Banks are safe. If you put money in a bank, you won't have to worry about losing it because banks and credit unions are federally insured. That means the federal government guarantees that if the bank goes out of business, the depositors will get their money back, up to $250,000 per depositor, per insured bank, for each account ownership category.[4]
3. When you are old enough to have a checking account, it is important that you keep good records. If you write

checks for more money than you have, your checks will bounce and you will be heavily fined.

4. While checks are a safe way to send money through the mail, living with cash on a day-to-day basis is a lot simpler because when it's gone, it's gone!

5. It is illegal, to say nothing of unethical, to write a check for more money than you know you have in the bank.

Automatic Teller Machines

The use of automatic teller machines (ATMs) is a privilege extended to experienced bank customers. Visiting the ATM on a regular basis can be hazardous to your wealth, because it is so easy to get money from one's account.

The best way an adult can make an ATM both convenient and safe is to visit rarely and track spending impeccably. Taking the time to go into the bank or credit union and deal with a real teller (unless of course your bank now charges a fee for such a privilege) takes extra time but does keep you in better contact with the whole concept of deposits and withdrawals.

Teaching Kids about ATMs

Looking at ATMs through a child's eye and mind will help you understand how necessary it is for her to understand how they work. ATMs are not money-making machines. An ATM card is not a magic key. There is a limit to the amount of money a person can withdraw from his account using an ATM.

Teach your kids that convenience often comes at a cost. Using ATM machines frequently can be costly because some of them charge a fee just to use the machine. Share experiences you may have had using an ATM when you were charged a fee to take out your own money!

What Kids Need to Know about ATMs

1. An ATM is like a robot. A bank can hire fewer tellers if it has an ATM to help customers with their money. ATMs are never late to work, never take a vacation, and rarely make mistakes.
2. Adults need a secret code called a PIN in order to get their money out of an ATM.
3. An ATM card is not a credit card. It's more like a "permission card" that allows a bank customer to withdraw some of his money without the need for a teller.
4. It is very important to keep track of all ATM withdrawals just as if you wrote a check or went into the bank and made an in-person withdrawal.
5. Most banks do not charge their own customers to use their ATMs. However, using an ATM owned by another bank will cost a fee.

Credit Cards

As a parent, you should think of a credit card as a live hand grenade. In your child's possession, it could go off when you least expect it and cause serious damage.

A child or teen does not need to have or use a credit card to learn everything there is to know about them. You want to teach your children that a credit card can be either used or abused. When used, it becomes a helpful tool that makes some things in life more convenient. When abused, credit cards—and the resulting debt—can make life miserable.

Credit card rules are simple. Never use a credit card to pay for something because you do not have enough money. If you use a credit card to secure a rental car or to pay for something you order over the phone or through the mail, always pay the balance in full within the grace period (the period of time when no interest will be due, typically twenty-five days). An adult needs only one all-purpose credit card.

Teaching Kids about Credit Cards

Use credit-card applications that come in the mail to explain interest rates and all of the terms and conditions. Talk about how credit cards have become the tender of choice in most retail establishments. These days only about 30 percent of those purchases are paid in full during the grace period. The rest become consumer debt because the cardholder pays only a small amount every month.

What Kids Need to Know about Credit Cards

1. A credit-card purchase creates a loan. You don't really own something you bought with a credit card until you pay the bill in full.
2. Responsible adults use a credit card as a helpful tool and to build a solid credit history, not to buy things

when they don't have enough money. That is why they need only one all-purpose credit card.

3. Abusing a credit card means using it to buy more things than you have the money to pay for. Carrying a credit-card balance from month to month is very expensive because of the high interest rates.

4. If you buy something with a credit card and then pay it off in low monthly payments, you will end up paying for it two or more times because of all the interest. A one-hundred-dollar MP3 player could end up costing three hundred dollars—and it would take many years to pay for it. And chances are that the player will not last as long as it takes to pay for it.

5. Credit-card debt is one of the reasons so many families have to file for bankruptcy in this country.

Debt

While we have already discussed debt in chapter 10, I would be remiss if I did not include it again here as an important part of building financial intelligence in your children. Go ahead and think of this as a review.

There are two kinds of debt: secured and unsecured. Unsecured debt is the killer because there is no collateral involved. If a person defaults on an unsecured obligation, the creditor comes after the person and his credit report. Unsecured debt is dangerous because when not paid in full in a very short period of time, it accrues large amounts of interest quickly. Unsecured debt should be avoided at all costs.

Secured debt involves collateral, and that is what makes it "safe debt." If you can't make the payments, the lender can take the collateral you put up to secure the loan in exchange for full payment. Secured debts include house loans and car loans.

Teaching Kids about Debt

Make sure your kids know the difference between secured and unsecured debt (see chap. 10).

If you have debts you regret, tell your kids about them—but only if you are comfortable doing so. You may want to admit that you've made some mistakes in the past without going into a lot of detail and that you are doing everything you can to pay off the debt quickly. Kids don't need to know all the details or to carry the burden of anxiety over family finances. Tell them enough to enlighten them but not so much as to cause them to become anxious.

While kids should find borrowing money abhorrent, if you decide to give your child a loan, require collateral. Make sure it is something as valuable as the amount he is borrowing and then take possession of it. The child should not have use of the collateral during the loan period in order to experience the full impact of debt.

Let's say, for example, your young teen must borrow fifty dollars for some reason and offers his electronic gaming equipment as collateral. Physically remove the item from his room and keep it in yours. Write up a promissory note, along with the condition that if payment is not made as agreed, the equipment becomes yours to sell in order to recover the debt.

Share stories and articles you read that pertain to consumer and other types of debt. Reflect on specific times you've felt like a slave because of debts you incurred, if indeed you have. If not, tell them about that too.

Make a chart of a debt-payment schedule that you feel comfortable sharing with your kids. If you have a mortgage, this might make a good visual. Post the payment schedule on the refrigerator, showing how much of the payment each month goes toward interest and how many more payments will be required to pay it in full. You'll be shocked, and so will your kids!

What Kids Need to Know about Debt

1. Unsecured debt is dangerous because if you have trouble making the payments you don't have a remedy.
2. Secured debts are safer debts because the value of the collateral provides security for both the borrower and the lender.
3. Never borrow money for something that will lose its value quickly or be used up in less than three years.
4. It is always best to avoid debt, but if you cannot, in the case of buying a house or a car, make sure the debt is secured and that you pay it off as quickly as possible.
5. Debt-free is a wonderful way to live. You can live on a lot less money if you have no debts, and you have a lot more options.

Consumerism

We do not want to glorify shopping and overconsumption, but we need to teach skills such as getting the best value for the best price and knowing how to return a product.

Much of this teaching can happen at home—prior to a shopping trip and away from the influence of the mall environment. The fact that your kids will be spending their own money will help them become savvy consumers. Kids are more reluctant to let go of their own money than they are to spend yours. When they spend their money, only to end up with a junky toy or other disappointing purchase, they learn a valuable lesson in consumerism.

You want to teach your kids how to match quality with need (don't spend a lot for a trendy item that will be here today and gone tomorrow), to keep receipts in case an adjustment needs to be made, to shop for the best value, to anticipate sales, and to shop out of season.

It takes two groups of people to make stores work: manufacturers who make things and consumers who buy what they make. Whenever you spend your money to buy something, you become a consumer. Some people become out-of-control consumers because they buy more than they need.

Responsible consumers find the best value for things they truly need or will use. Responsible consumers comparison shop. They check different stores to find the best price for the item they need. Or they simply use a comparison shopping website and compare prices. They compare features and guarantees and shipping charges for online purchases. They read reviews. They do research to find out which products are recommended by experts.

Careful consumers don't make decisions hastily. They take time to think so they make the best choice. Sometimes the cheapest choice is not the best choice. If you are shopping for something that needs to last a short time, like a swimming suit that you're going to outgrow before next summer, you should probably look for the cheapest price. This is called matching quality with need.

On the other hand, if something needs to last a long time (like an appliance), it would be silly to buy the cheapest one if that means it won't be reliable. Paying a little bit more to get something that will last would be a much better choice.

As a consumer, you should expect satisfaction. That means if you buy something and it doesn't work or doesn't fit right, you take it back for an exchange or a refund. Smart consumers are polite and courteous. Always treat store employees the way you would like them to treat you.

Teaching Kids to Be Responsible Consumers

When a child is with you at the supermarket, teach him to compare prices. Most stores these days disclose the per-unit price, making it simple for a child to see which box of cereal is the better value.

Help your kids evaluate the quality of a product before making a purchase.

Allow kids to observe you handling a customer service situation where you need to return an item or make an exchange. Teach them to save their receipts and to understand store policies about such matters.

Help your children comparison shop once they've saved the money for that new bike or special outfit. Go to several stores and write down prices and features. Spend time comparing. Find out if the item of interest will be going on sale any time soon. Encourage them to sleep on their decision for at least twenty-four hours. Minds do change!

Teach kids how to match quality with need. A growing girl doesn't need the quality of a hundred-dollar pair of shoes. She won't wear them long enough to warrant the investment. A single grandmother wouldn't need an extra-capacity, heavy-duty washing machine, but a family with twelve kids would.

What Kids Need to Know about Consumerism

1. Responsible consumers spend their money wisely and make smart choices.
2. Consumers have the right to full satisfaction. If you are not happy with the quality or performance of something you buy, return it for a refund or exchange.
3. The best value may not always be the item with the cheapest price.
4. Buying things secondhand or used is a great way to get what you need at a bargain price.

Credit Reports and Credit Scores

Credit reports and credit scores are a fact of life. There's no way to avoid them, so the best course of action is to make sure you and your kids have clean, positive credit histories.

A credit score, a computer-generated three-digit score that statistically determines how likely you are to pay your bills, is used for more these days than simply qualifying a person for new debt. Many employers look at a credit score to learn of the job candidate's true character. Late payments and credit charge-offs say a lot about the way a person conducts his or her life.

Insurance companies, employers, and landlords typically request a person's credit score before making a decision.

Teaching Kids about Credit Reports and Credit Scores

You can teach kids a lot about life and consequences of behavior with a credit report. Order a copy of your own report (if it does not have information you wish to keep private from your kids; if it does, ask the credit bureau to send you a sample report) and go over it with them. It will look like Greek in the beginning, but persistence will pay off. The report will come with instructions on how to read it and how to report any erroneous information.

Your children will need to establish their own credit. I suggest they do so by about age twenty, but no earlier than age eighteen. Doing so will create a credit history file in which their credit report will be housed, a report that will stay with them for life.

Teach your children that a credit report is like a report card. Once negative information such as late payments on bills are on a credit report, they stay there for many years. It is impossible to have them "fixed" or erased. You can, however, have incorrect information removed, and you should. You wouldn't want false information to keep you from renting an apartment or getting a job.

What Kids Need to Know about Credit Reports and Credit Scores

1. A credit report is a financial report card. It is like a permanent school record. Every adult has a credit record that is kept by a company called a credit bureau or a credit reporting agency.
2. When you apply for a credit card, a credit report is opened in your name and kept in the files of the credit bureaus.
3. No one can look at your credit report without your written permission. When you apply for a job or an apartment, the company owner or landlord may ask your permission to see your credit report.
4. Because a credit report shows how you are with paying your bills and keeping your word, it serves as a character report.
5. Once a year go over your credit report (order it from the bureau) to make sure all the information is correct. It will come with instructions on how to make corrections to erroneous information.

Compound Interest

Teaching kids about compound interest gives meaning to the act of saving and investing money. That's what makes it fun.

Compound interest has a remarkable effect on money you save for a long time, as demonstrated in the chart that follows.

Michael and Justin both decided to save one thousand dollars a year. Michael got excited and started right away. He kept to his plan for eight years, and then he stopped adding one thousand dollars to his account every year. But he didn't take his money out of the account. He left it in the account, which earned 10 percent interest compounded annually (a rate we have not seen for some time, but let's just use this for illustration purposes right now and pray those rates return someday soon).

Age	Michael Invests	Total with Compounded Interest	Justin Invests	Total with Compounded Interest
22	$1,000	$1,100	0	
23	1,000	2,310	0	
24	1,000	3,641	0	
25	1,000	5,105	0	
26	1,000	6,716	0	
27	1,000	8,488	0	
28	1,000	10,437	0	
29	1,000	12,581	0	
30	0	13,839	1,000	$1,100
31	0	15,223	1,000	2,310
32	0	16,745	1,000	3,641
33	0	18,420	1,000	5,105
34	0	20,262	1,000	6,716
35	0	22,882	1,000	8,488

Age	Michael Invests	Total with Compounded Interest	Justin Invests	Total with Compounded Interest
36	0	24,517	1,000	10,437
37	0	26,969	1,000	12,581
38	0	29,666	1,000	14,939
39	0	32,633	1,000	17,533
40	0	35,896	1,000	20,386
41	0	39,486	1,000	23,525
42	0	43,435	1,000	26,978
43	0	47,779	1,000	30,776
44	0	52,557	1,000	39,954
45	0	57,813	1,000	39,549
46	0	63,594	1,000	44,604
47	0	69,953	1,000	50,164
48	0	76,948	1,000	56,280
49	0	84,643	1,000	63,008
50	0	93,107	1,000	70,409
51	0	102,418	1,000	78,550
52	0	112,660	1,000	87,505
53	0	123,926	1,000	97,356
54	0	136,319	1,000	108,192
55	0	149,951	1,000	120,111
56	0	164,946	1,000	133,282
57	0	181,441	1,000	147,644
58	0	199,585	1,000	163,508
59	0	219,544	1,000	180,959
60	0	241,498	1,000	200,155
61	0	265,648	1,000	221,271
62	0	292,213	1,000	244,498
63	0	321,434	1,000	270,048
64	0	353,577	1,000	298,153
65	0	388,935	1,000	329,068
Total	$8,000	$388,935	$36,000	$329,068

While it is not recommended that anyone set out to be as foolish as Michael and stop saving after only eight years, even that is much more intelligent than starting later or procrastinating for eight years like Justin.

Even with the consistency of Justin's savings program, once he got over his procrastination (he added one thousand dollars a year for thirty-six years!), he was unable to catch the growth of Michael's account. That's because of the phenomenon of compound interest. The moral of the story is this: Sooner is better than later.

Here's another scenario to consider. If your child saves just one dollar a day from birth on, invested at 6 percent interest compounded monthly for sixty-five years, his investment will become $2,379,807. That's what happens when $23,401 is exposed to growth through compound interest. Think about that for a few minutes. Saving one dollar a day is not out of reach for most families. Of course, you would accumulate this daily amount until you have enough to open an investment account and then add to it monthly ($30) or annually ($365). Now imagine if this investment account returned on average 12 percent per year. The end amount becomes $7,276,466.

One word of friendly advice: Start now!

Teaching Kids about Compound Interest

Here is a great story[5] to tell your kids that will illustrate the miracle of compound interest.

In 1492, Christopher Columbus decided he was going to save for retirement. He had one penny ($0.01), and he knew he could earn 6 percent every year on his money. He put the penny in his left pocket and placed the interest ($0.01 x 6% = $0.0006) into his right pocket for safekeeping. He never added anything to his original penny in his left pocket. Yet the interest accumulated year after year in his right pocket.

Chris is a very healthy guy. He lives until 2012—520 years later—and he decides to retire. So he takes his one penny from his left pocket and adds it to the simple interest in his right pocket. Do you know how much Mr. Columbus has now?

The interest in his right pocket adds up to about $0.30 (520 years x $0.0006 = $.3084). Along with his original penny from his left pocket, he has thirty-one cents on which to retire. Not very good planning!

What could Chris have done differently?

Let's assume Chris was much more astute about investing because he knew about the miracle of compound interest. Instead of putting the interest in his right pocket, he put it in his left pocket with the original penny—the principal. Over the years, he would earn the same 6 percent interest on the original penny and also on the accumulated interest in his left pocket.

At the end of year one, he had $0.0106 in his left pocket (the original penny plus the 6 percent interest). At the end of year two, he had $0.011236 ($0.0106 plus 6 percent interest). At the end of year three, he had $0.01191 ($0.011236 plus 6 percent interest). This is called compounding and continued for Chris for 520 years.

So in this scenario, how much did good ol' Chris accumulate for retirement by taking advantage of compound interest? The answer is somewhat more to Chris's liking. At the end of 520 years, with the original penny at 6 percent interest compounded annually, Chris has $144,228,118,378.68 (that's 144 billion, 228 million, 118 thousand, 378 dollars, and 68 cents!) That's a lot of pocket change.[6]

None of us will live that long, but all of us will have more than one penny to invest.

What Kids Need to Know about Compound Interest

1. Compound interest makes your savings and investments grow. It is important to leave money alone so it can grow. If you withdraw it, the growth stops.
2. Compound interest is like a teammate you can always count on. Twenty-four hours a day, seven days a week, it is earning money for you. It works weekends, holidays, and nights. It never takes a day off, and it earns just as much for you on the days when you are sick as when you are well.

13

neutralize the glamour of easy spending

There is no reasonable way to shield your children from the glitz and glamour of credit. It's everywhere with all its seduction and allure. So if you cannot shield, neutralize!

Years ago I watched an effective television documentary in which juvenile delinquents went into prisons, drug-treatment centers, and the like to observe the dark side of the life they were heading toward. The intention was to scare them out of their wits—to scare them straight.

In the same way these kids were jolted by reality, you can scare your kids out of a life of consumer debt by revealing the lies behind the glamour.

Think of consumer credit as a stalker on the loose who is after kids. You know this stalker is out there, what he looks like, how he operates, and when he's most likely to strike.

Your best line of defense is to describe him in detail to your kids and tell them everything you know about him so they can be prepared with a counterattack.

Tell Stories

There is nothing as effective as true stories when it comes to scaring kids about the dangers of consumer debt. You've read a few such stories in this book. There are, unfortunately, thousands more where those came from.

From time to time I've read stories in newspapers or magazines about how individuals and families went nuts with credit. I have drawers full of such clippings that tell of ruined lives.

Both Jeremy and Josh have worked in our newsletter publishing office over the years, and that has given them plenty of opportunities to read some horror stories—and also some success stories—about consumer debt. It's impossible to work in the Debt-Proof Living office without getting a consumer-debt wake-up call.

Share credit horror stories with your kids as often as you can (it's best to stick to stories you read in newspapers, newsletters, or other published sources rather than gossip). Let your teen or older child draw conclusions and suggest what would have been a better course of action. Let them be the ones to point out how foolish it is to live beyond your means. Follow up with an explanation that when people are not financially knowledgeable, they are easy marks for the debt trap.

Explain Credit-Card Applications

Credit-card applications that fill your mailbox make great teaching material. Have a few handy when an opportunity arises to go over them with your older kids and teens.

Using critical analysis, assess everything about each mailing piece: the envelope copy, the letter inside, the greeting, the promises, and the flattery. Don't forget about the small print. These days the small print brings new meaning to "small," and many companies have gone to pale gray ink for the small print, making it even more difficult to read. It would be worth your time to enlarge a few of these applications on a photocopy machine so you can easily read them.

Have your kids highlight all the lies and phrases of flattery they can find in the letters that come with the credit-card applications. Check the envelope too. Explain that it's human nature to enjoy this kind of praise, but it's wrong to use flattery to manipulate.

Here are excerpts from the ten applications we received at our house in just one week. Be sure to notice how they drip with flattery and manipulation:

- We want your business now! We want you to carry our most exclusive credit card because you've earned it with your excellent credit record.
- Every bank with a premium card wants your business. But we want it more! You'll be able to spend as you please!
- Your satisfaction is guaranteed!
- This is just our way of thanking you for your business.

- You are prequalified! You're invited to request the card that reflects the financial standing you've achieved.

- Why settle for an ordinary credit card when you can request [name of card], which gives you the power, prestige, and acceptance you deserve?

- Because privilege speaks for itself, because you've earned it! Your success and accomplishments deserve recognition.

- There is no better value on the market today for financially savvy individuals like you. Due to your superior record of financial management, your excellent financial standing will be reflected in exceptional purchasing power.

- Travel and shop with the security of [name of card]. These privileges are simply not available to everyone. So it should come as no surprise that you are in a position to enjoy the very best we have to offer!

Search out all the statements that aren't true and challenge them. Example: "The more you spend, the more you'll save!" Truth: You cannot save by spending. The more you spend, the more you spend!

How about this one: "Use our credit card at any of the over 271,000 ATM machines and you'll have the cash you need!" Truth: Taking a cash advance on a credit card represents a very expensive loan. You'll end up with more debt than you know!

Notice how many applications use words such as *spending limit*, *cash*, *power*, *prestige*, *unique services*, *privilege*, and *you deserve*. Notice the clever use of precious metals to make us think certain credit cards are more prestigious, which must mean we're more prestigious to be invited to accept them. First there was silver, gold, and platinum. The latest is titanium.

Have your children find all the times the word *debt* is used. (You could safely offer a ten-dollar reward for each occurrence your kids can find without having to worry much. The word *debt* is mysteriously missing from credit-card applications.) Credit-card applications make it appear that carrying a balance from month to month is some kind of benefit or privilege.

Talk about the interest rates, the late and over-limit fees, the terms under which the rules can be changed.

If you have access to a financial calculator (there are many credit-card calculators on the internet) or a computer program such as Quicken, play around with what-ifs using the terms of your credit-card applications.

"What if I used this credit card to buy [fill in the blank] for [fill in the amount] and made the minimum payments required? How many years would I be in debt and how much interest would I end up paying?" Now estimate how long you will enjoy the item of consideration.

This is such an amazing exercise that you'll secretly thank the credit-card companies for sending such effective anti-debt teaching tools.

Once you've finished tearing apart the phony flattery and exposing the truth of an application, don't throw it in the trash. I have a better idea to help you and your kids put a fun close on your critical examination. Tear up the application and the letter into tiny pieces and place them in the pre-addressed, postage-paid envelope that accompanied the offer. Seal it and send it back to the company. That is a good way to say, "No, thank you!"

Never miss an opportunity to expose the danger of credit-card debt to your children.

Expose the "Nothing Down, No Payments" Mystery

Perhaps you've wondered about the currently popular "nothing down, no payments, no interest" kind of advertising. You'll see this in newspaper ads and store windows, particularly around the holidays. What a seductive yet deceitful come-on! You must carefully read the fine print to figure this out, and even then it can be confusing.

I was so curious that I actually went into a store advertising such a "wonderful" opportunity and asked the credit manager to explain it to me.

First, there is a qualifying process. Only those customers with pristine credit reports can qualify. That alone puts the retailer/lender in a great position, but typically people with pristine credit are not drawn by the lure of something for nothing.

Next, the offer is for a limited time. Those "no payments" are for the first six months or until January of the next year—something like that.

Even though it appears there is no obligation on the part of the customer, that could not be further from the truth. The customer must sign the credit application, promising to pay an outrageous interest rate (usually the maximum allowed by state law, which can be as high as 28 to 32 percent) with the understanding that the interest is deferred for the initial period.

Now here's the kicker: If the customer doesn't pay the entire amount due within that deferred interest period ("And not one minute late," according to the credit manager), interest becomes due immediately and is retroactive to the date of purchase.

Here's the reason stores love to advertise this way. Most people who want these deals can't qualify. But the advertisement catches their attention. Within seconds, they feel entitled to have new furniture, an electronic item, or even a new car. Emotionally, they've moved it in and are enjoying it. So when they get the bad news, they're ripe to fall for a more expensive deal, which the salesperson is quick to offer.

Now let's talk about the people who do qualify for the program and go ahead with the offer. At least 78 percent, according to the credit manager I spoke with, fail to make the entire payment by the deadline. Whoops. Then the agreement they signed kicks in.

Those customers are stuck paying high interest retroactively back to the day they signed the agreement. Of course, this means hefty monthly payments on furniture that's no longer new, a computer that's already obsolete, or some other thing that's now old hat.

This kind of nothing-down offer is very lucrative for the store because it gets a lot of people to come in. When only a small percentage can qualify for the offer, they shuffle the rest into some other credit plan that nets the store even more money. There are many people out there who will do most anything to get something right now as long as they can pay for it later.

Whenever you see this kind of advertising, you can create a teachable moment by asking your kids how they think that works. "If you owned that store, would you be worried about letting someone take furniture with nothing down, no interest, and no payments?"

Deglamourize Home Shopping

Here's a great way to get your older kids to think realistically about home shopping television and online shopping sites.

Start with a credit-card application from your mailbox. Have your child figure out the terms. Now pretend that you are going on a shopping spree with this phony-baloney credit card. Tune into one of the home shopping networks on television, go online, or grab a mail-order catalog and go wild!

The rule is you can "buy" whatever you see but only for a predetermined period of time. Write down everything you've "ordered" with your pretend card. At the end of the time, add up the total cost plus the shipping and handling of all the stuff you ordered. Now get your financial calculator and assess the "damage."

Using the total as the balance and the payment terms on the application, find out how many years it is going to take you to pay for this shopping spree. Whew! You'll be mighty glad this was only a game. And just think of all the stuff you won't have to take care of—or return because you've had a reality check.

In the chart that follows, take a look at what I "bought" in only twenty minutes when I went on this kind of phony shopping spree.

Item	Price	Shipping/Handling
16-piece gem set	$111.46	$5.99
14K gold ring setting	244.08	7.99
Shoe laces (3 pairs)	11.87	3.97
Pearl leaf bracelet	170.00	4.97
18K cherub charm bracelet	704.50	4.97
Praying angel ring	147.50	4.97
Fleur-de-lis 18K necklace	422.00	4.97
18K angel pendant	56.25	3.97
18K lady/orchid necklace	2,154.00	9.97
18K cross pendant	65.00	3.97
18K gold cable chain	397.00	5.97
9-inch 18K anklet	186.00	4.97

I "bought" $4,736 in home shopping merchandise of marginal quality in twenty minutes. Pretending that I put this on an 18.99 percent interest credit card that requires minimum payments of 3 percent of the outstanding balance (or ten dollars, whichever is more), here is the damage I did in just twenty minutes: It would take more than nineteen years (234 months to be exact) of minimum monthly payments to pay back a total of $9,793, including interest.

Expose DVD and Game Clubs

The advertisements are very tempting. What kid these days wouldn't be interested in getting four Disney movies on DVD for $1.99 each? Or ten tunes for a buck? While many music, movie, and book clubs offer an excellent service to mature adults, kids have a difficult time seeing through the promise of something for nothing.

Save a few of the club offerings and read the membership details with your kids. Here's what kids need to know: Even though the initial order is really inexpensive (nearly free!), there's usually a significant shipping and handling fee per DVD or item that will show up in the future. That fee per item is often about the same as it would cost to buy a similar product in a discount store. But the kicker is that by accepting the initial offer, you agree to the terms of the club. Sometimes you are obligated to buy a certain number of selections at the full price.

Making it even more difficult for kids, some of these clubs have what is called a "negative response" feature. By accepting the initial offer, you have agreed to purchase the monthly selection, and you'll receive it every month along with a bill for the full price plus shipping and handling—unless you are careful to return the card that says you don't want it.

All of these things should make mail-order music and book clubs off-limits for kids. By saving their money and watching for sales, kids can generally beat the club prices, even taking into consideration the initial offering, and get just the titles they really want.

The best way to neutralize the glamour of consumer credit is to face it head-on and expose it. Talking openly and honestly with your kids about the pitfalls will remove the hard candy shell to reveal the bitter pill beneath.

14

the preschool years

Children under the age of five don't possess the cognitive skills necessary to make a connection between money and value. In fact, preschoolers have little, if any, understanding of money at all.

Youngsters of this age don't understand the theory behind saving because they have no concept of time. They much prefer a nickel to a dime because it's bigger.

While attempting to teach abstract financial ideas to children so young would be of little benefit, it is important to understand that during the first five years of life a child develops much of his or her moral intelligence.

Kids are shaped at the very beginning of life by the way their parents live. They are ever-attentive watchers of grown-up behaviors. They take their cues from what they see and hear. What they do best is observe and imitate.

While they don't understand the meaning of abstract ideas, even toddlers can learn frugality by seeing that we are not wasteful and that we are thankful for what we have. Children grow morally by learning how to be with others and how to behave in the world.

If you want your children to grow up with healthy attitudes about money, and what it can and cannot do, start demonstrating those attitudes and behaviors from day one.

Do's for Preschoolers

Let them observe Mommy and Daddy taking good care of their money.

Let them see you and their older siblings using money as an ordinary and normal part of life.

Let them see you giving money to others. Make sure they catch you being generous with others and sharing what you have.

Let them see you deposit money in the bank.

Let them see the way you pay for groceries with cash. Teach them that money is important in our lives because we can exchange it for things we need and want.

Talk about money as casually as you talk about things such as sports and laundry.

Use coins to teach your preschooler to count. This acknowledges kids' curiosity about money.

Talk about the different shapes and colors of items in the store. Doing so gives little ones something to do instead of wanting everything they see.

Allow your little one, while riding in the grocery cart, to hold the coupons or the list. Talk about planning, saving, and finding the best value.

Say, "We don't choose to spend our money that way" more often than you say, "We can't afford it."

Remember that preschoolers are listening to and learning from everything they hear you say and see you do.

Use coins to teach the different denominations. Three- and four-year-olds can learn to put the pennies into one cup, the nickels into another, and so on.

Visit the library or park with your preschooler more often than the market or mall.

Give rewards of hugs and praise—not money. Creating the expectation of cash payment at every turn is a habit you'll regret in adolescence.

Monitor television time and opt for noncommercial DVDs and videos when possible.

Let preschoolers participate in household chores to enjoy the security of belonging—not to get paid.

Intervene between advertisers and your kids. Preschoolers can't always tell when a television show ends and an ad begins.

Let your children count potatoes, oranges, and other items as you put them in the bag at the grocery store.

Don'ts for Preschoolers

Don't confuse children's healthy attitudes about money by using credit cards and ATMs when they're around.

Don't argue about money in front of your kids.

Don't allow preschoolers to be only takers. Help them find ways to give to others.

Don't overindulge your preschoolers. It's healthy for them to yearn just a little from time to time. It will help prepare them for real life when they cannot have everything they want.

Don't use money to bribe or manipulate. Kids pick up on that quickly.

Don't let your kids see or hear you worry about money.

Don't let your kids mistake love for money. Little surprises and gifts of money are expressions of affection, but very young children see them as substitutes.

Don't overexpose toddlers and preschoolers to stores and supermarkets.

Don't forget that too much commercial television creates unhealthy doses of desire.

Don't be surprised when despite your best efforts your preschoolers still want it all. It's natural. Young kids forget quickly what they didn't get—but ugly attitudes of entitlement go on and on.

15

ages six through nine

by now your children have moved into their elementary school years. They are reading; they understand simple abstract ideas. But that's not all. Your children have become part of that important demographic group of kiddy consumers we mentioned in chapter 9—kids who will determine how billions of dollars are spent on them in this year alone. An entire industry is focusing its attention on your kids.

By age six your children have become very much a part of the real world. They are keenly aware of money and what they believe it can do to make them happy. Now is the perfect time for you to start teaching.

Make an Allowance

Most six-year-olds know about allowances, and they want their own money. You may be able to put them off for a few more years—even until they are old enough to go into a formal salary program such as our family plan (see chap. 4). But why wait if they are ready for some hands-on learning now? A simple allowance program will fit perfectly into these interim years before they are ready to go on salary.

Think of it this way. If putting your children on salary when they are older is like letting them swim in the deep end, then giving them an allowance now is like letting them practice in the shallow end of the pool—complete with water wings, swimming lessons, and you, their attentive lifeguard.

At this age, kids are teachable, eager to learn, and still believe everything adults tell them. You will have wonderful opportunities to pass on your values to your elementary-aged kids as you closely guide them through simple lessons on needs versus wants, giving, and saving for future purchases.

How Much and How Often?

The exact allowance amount will depend on your particular situation. As you are deciding on a figure, remember that you want these years to be an understated precursor of what is to come when your kids are older and they go on salary.

Some families set allowances according to age—fifty cents to one dollar for each year of age. That method automatically determines when and how much to increase.

At this age, kids do better with close supervision and short time frames, so receiving their allowance weekly is best. Set a specific day of the week to pay allowances so everyone knows what to expect—no surprises, no misunderstandings.

Tied to Chores?

Some experts say allowances should be the payment children receive for doing their chores and assigned jobs. No work? No pay. They say an allowance must be earned.

Others say that as citizens of the "family community," where each family member has the right to share in its rewards, income, and responsibilities, children should receive an allowance as their share of the family income. They say an allowance should not be the payment for chores and assigned jobs. But, they add, with privilege comes responsibility. Citizens must do chores and jobs because they are part of the community—not for payment. That's just what good citizens do.

I agree with the second group. Children learn responsibility when they perform chores that are commensurate with their age and abilities. But they're still kids. And they will forget or do an unacceptable job now and then. It's unfair to dock their pay or withhold their allowance. Handle the matter in a way that fits the infraction.

A third allowance alternative combines these options. Give your kids a base allowance that is quite low and assign them regular chores that are separate from the allowance. Then post a list of optional jobs that are available for additional pay. Example: Wash Mom's car—$5.00. This variation seems to cover all the bases. The children can count on a portion of the community income, they are responsible to work for the community, and they have an incentive to earn more money.

You will recall from a previous chapter that we did not dock or withhold our kids' salaries if they failed to do their chores or did them unacceptably. We issued citations in those situations, and the greater the offense, the higher the fine. Like getting a speeding ticket, it's a painful way to learn a lesson.

Giving and Saving

Your kids need to begin living the values you're teaching them about giving and saving part of the money they receive. Enforcing these values through the allowance system gets those values operating in their lives from a very young age.

Jars are popular with kids this age and are perfect substitutes for bank accounts. In one family, each child has four jars marked to show the deposit allocations:

Giving: 10 percent

Long-term savings: 10 percent

Short-term savings: 40 percent

Spend now: 40 percent

Their plan says that long-term savings are for college or something far away. Short-term savings are for something significant such as a new bike or toy. "Spend now" is money the child can spend right away.

Another family has a community giving jar. Everyone puts 10 percent in the central collection center. When the giving jar contains a tidy sum, they call a community meeting to present ideas of where to give the money. Then the family votes and makes the delivery.

Community Taxes

There's no time like when they're young to teach kids about taxes and how the real world operates. Here's one clever idea, one that every family should consider.

The family who shared this idea with me told how the parents instituted the taxing system as part of their family's plan. As a family, they voted for a 15 percent across-the-board income tax. Everyone agreed that on allowance day each person would have his or her taxes withheld and deposited directly into the family's tax jar, which was located in a central place in the house where everyone could watch the funds grow. Each year, the family voted how that year's taxes would be spent. The first year the contents of the tax jar went toward the family vacation.

I cannot think of a better way to teach kids about how the real world operates than to allow them to experience a representative democracy in action. My advice is that everyone in the family who draws an allowance or salary from the household income should be taxed. That includes the parents, provided they receive an allowance from the household income, money they can call their own. (See more on spousal allowances in *Debt-Proof Your Marriage*.) The money should be used in a way that benefits all tax-paying citizens of the family community.

Spending

While your kids should be able to spend a portion of their allowance as they decide, they also need supervision. Some parents require that they give permission before a purchase is made.

Kids should have a clear understanding of family values regarding what they can buy and what's not allowed in their home. One family wrote that a daughter used her spending money to buy a tube top—something that was clearly not acceptable. She lost the garment and her money on that poor choice. You'll especially want to monitor your younger children's spending closely.

Loan-Free Zone

You will thank me a thousand times over if you follow my suggestion to create a hard-and-fast rule with your kids: no unsecured debt. Period. Never. Don't even ask.

This rule will kick in when you're standing in the middle of the store and your child suddenly wants something but realizes he left his money at home. It's difficult to say no when it would be so easy to cover the cost just until you got home. But if you do, you've just changed the rules. The answer should be a kind yet firm no.

Hold them to the rule, and you'll be surprised how quickly they learn to adhere to it.

16

age ten through teen

Your kids want independence and freedom. You want them to take responsibility for their actions. They want decision-making power. You want them to make the right choices. They are struggling to break away. You can't bear the thought of letting go. Welcome to adolescence.

It has been nearly twenty-six years since we designed our Financially Confident Kid Plan (chaps. 4 and 5). We have had plenty of time to evaluate, and the results are in.

In all its simplicity, our plan was successful—I mean hugely, wonderfully successful. The plan accomplished its purpose. We put our kids in charge of their own spending decisions. We gave them a significant salary, lots of financial responsibility, and stepped back into the position of advisors, even as we were getting our own financial house in order.

Things are different now than they were in the mid-1980s when we took Uncle Harvey's idea and developed it into a unique money plan for our family. Consumer credit wasn't as available then as it is now—especially to teens and young adults. We would have thought the internet was something you attached between two trees to make a hammock. The commercialization of our lives was not so intense.

Still, I know that our financial plan—because it is so simple, logical, and adaptable to any parent-child situation—can do for your family what it did for ours. This is a reasonable way to eliminate the power struggles that clog the channels of communication between teens and their parents.

If your children have been on an allowance system, moving into a salaried plan will be the next logical step. If your kids are new to any kind of allowance program or financial responsibility, don't hesitate to jump in now and get them up to speed.

It is at this point in your kids' lives—age ten or eleven—that I recommend beginning your version of our plan. Even if a child is well into his teens, it's only too late if you don't start now.

A Written Plan

I have a theory about plans. If they're not written down, they're only a dream. You don't want your kids' financial futures floating around in some dream state. That's why your kids' financial plan should be a written document. There are other benefits to writing your plan:

- It becomes visually symbolic.
- It creates authority.

- It organizes your ideas and values.
- It will give your kids something to show their kids (think family heirloom).

The equipment you use can be as simple or as elaborate as you want, but before you run out and spend a fortune on a leather-bound portfolio, remember that you can always upgrade later. All you need in the beginning is a notebook.

Divide your notebook into sections for the mission statement and rules regarding salaries, payment method, mandatory disbursements, spending, record keeping, borrowing, and termination. You'll also want a section for each of your children where you can record their yearly responsibility lists and salary histories. I'm sure there are as many ways to set this up as there are families. The only way you can get it wrong is if you don't try.

The Basic Plan Provisions

Mission statement. Develop a written statement that describes the purpose of your plan and how you intend to accomplish it. Writing a mission statement is a powerful process. It takes all those ideas floating around in your head and turns them into something clear and useful. Developing your own unique purpose in this simple way will create a sense of excitement and adventure. It may take a few minutes; it could take a few weeks.

Responsibility list. This is a detailed list of all the items you will no longer buy for your child. A ten-year-old's list should be quite different from that of a seventeen-year-old. The theory is that you keep adding responsibilities so that by the last year on the plan the child's list includes everything, with the possible exception of at-home food and shelter.

Salary. This is the sum of money you give to your child that covers all the items you would normally buy for him and that are on the responsibility list.

One reason you need to start planning many months in advance is so you know what you spend on your kids. Trust me, you'll be amazed. As money dribbles out of your pockets and purses, it doesn't seem like much. But just start keeping track. Even with all of this information, you'll still have to estimate and finally just pick a number. But at least you'll be in the ballpark.

Once you are a few years down the road, the monthly salary is going to be significant. If you add up all the clothes, cosmetics, haircuts, yearbooks, movies, school supplies, gifts, gasoline, dates, sports, lessons, trips, books, DVDs, cellphones, ringtones, and on and on that you buy for your kids and teens in the course of a year, you'll be looking at a substantial number. Divide that by twelve, and it's not unthinkable that an older teen's monthly salary will be $150, $200, or even more, depending on your lifestyle and situation. It is important that you be as realistic as possible in estimating your kids' expenses.

Payment method. Salary should be paid on a monthly basis in cash. It requires more responsibility and forces the child to make better plans if it comes less often but in a larger quantity. And it seems like a more serious amount of money. One hundred dollars a month is more dramatic than twenty-five dollars a week.

Mandatory disbursements. Our rule was that all salaried individuals must give and save. You can hardly go wrong by following the classic 10-10-80 formula (10 percent given away, 10 percent to savings, 80 percent to live on).

Spending. We allowed our boys to make their own spending decisions for 80 percent of their salary. In the first year, all the items on their responsibility list were "wants." There was nothing they had to buy, but if they wanted anything on the list, they used their money.

As your children grow and the lists (and salaries) expand, you will likely add clothes, haircuts, school supplies, and many other things to their lists. While they are making the decisions regarding the items on the lists, there should be a clear expectation that they will get haircuts and buy the required school supplies.

Record keeping. Kids must keep a written spending record and a spending plan. We neglected to include this important rule in our plan, and if we had it to do again, this would be mandatory. At the time, we didn't know how important it is to know where the money goes. Enforce this rule to create a lifelong habit, not so your child is accountable to you for every nickel spent. The spending record becomes the tool to create the spending plan, which will be enormously important as kids begin buying their own clothes and other life essentials.

Spending records will also become important if there is a complaint along the way that a child's responsibilities exceed his salary. Without a detailed record of where his money is going, you won't know if there really is a discrepancy or simply an overspending problem.

Borrowing. Unless it's a matter of health or personal safety, there should be no salary advances or borrowing. Loans are not an alternative except in exceptional situations and then only if the loan has collateral. You want your plan as loophole-free as possible.

Termination. Don't forget to decide when your salary plan will end. We continued through the summer after high school, but this would be a matter unique to each family's situation. Some families wean their kids off salary gradually as they begin to find employment outside the home.

Parental hands-off. Parents must pledge to follow the hands-off rule. This is the most difficult provision for the parents but one of the kids' favorites.

By letting your kids make their own spending decisions without your interference, you empower them with confidence. As a parent who's been there, let me tell you how difficult it will be to keep your mouth shut. But you must. Your kids will never learn the truth about consequences if they aren't allowed to make mistakes. Just be thankful they'll be making them while the consequences are not long-lasting or earth-shattering.

Getting Started

The ideal time to put kids on salary is when they are young enough to be impressed but mature enough to reason and understand simple financial concepts. The ideal age seems to be about ten or eleven. When in doubt, sooner is better than later. It really is ideal to get kids started on a salary plan before they reach adolescence. Start while they are still compliant, think their parents are terrific, and don't talk back. They'll make the transition into adolescence so smoothly that you'll wonder if everything is normal.

Explaining the System

Most kids are more than speechless when they learn about a family plan that will allow them to make their own spending decisions. When they hear how much money they will be managing, they are eager to get going. It's important to stress that it's not all privilege—a great deal of responsibility is expected. They need to know just how much trust you are placing in them, that you trust them to handle large sums of money and make wise choices.

The Launch

Going on salary is a very important step for a kid—a rite of passage. If you treat the event in a memorable way, it will take on even more significance. A special dinner or certificate can mark the start of this new season as each of your children become full-fledged family money managers.

Annual Expansion

At least once a year (more often if your kids are older when they start), sit down with your children and add as many more items to their responsibility lists as possible. As you add more and more things to the lists, more responsibility is required, and more learning will happen.

By the time they reach their senior year of high school, their salaries should be at a level to cover all senior expenses such as a class ring, prom, a yearbook, and a senior trip.

Clearly, this is not a one-size-fits-all-families kind of money plan. There are many variables. But the basic plan is adaptable to all situations.

Q & A

Everyone who hears about this kind of plan for the first time has questions. Here are some of the most frequently asked:

Q: I can't imagine giving my ten-year-old fifty dollars and expecting him to know what to do with it, let alone have anything left next week at this time.

A: Of course you wouldn't do that without a great deal of preparation (chap. 4) and some very clear-cut rules. At age ten, your son may not be mature enough to jump in at this more advanced level. Why not put him into a more structured allow-ance program (see chap. 15) for a year or so in which he receives a weekly allowance with fewer responsibilities and more supervision?

Q: Doesn't this salary program constitute a free hand-out that will only encourage kids to turn into adults who think they don't have to work for a living?

A: No. If you've read all the chapters, you know I be-lieve children should do chores and regular work around the house, not for pay but because they are citizens of the family community.

I believe that children are their parents' financial responsibility. While some think that kids need to get outside jobs to pay for things they want, I don't agree. I believe childhood is a time to learn about life, not to be employed. Kids need to be kids, to participate fully in school and become educated.

We didn't keep it a secret from our boys that they would be expected to get jobs during the summer after their senior year in high school. They had plenty of notice for when their salaries would end. There were no complaints, no problems. They both got their jobs, we stopped paying salaries, and the transition was seamless. They were pleased because the salaries we were giving them were far less than what they earned on their part-time jobs.

Our salary structure did not allow for a lavish lifestyle. Actually, it taught our boys to be quite frugal—a lifestyle they chose for themselves. The salary we turned over to them was the same money we had used to buy things for them. We simply transferred it from our care into theirs.

Q: Our son is twelve. We like for him to go to camp twice a year. If we include the cost of camp in his salary, does he get to choose whether or not to go?

A: That's the way the plan works. If this were a case in which he was eager to go, you wouldn't have a problem. But if he's going because you make him go, you'd better not include that in the salary. If you pay for his camp, you retain control over him in that area.

When we faced the camp situation with Josh, he wanted to go to camp as badly as we wanted him to go. But camp was a little pricey, and his salary was none too extravagant. We compromised by matching his contribution, which means we paid half. We didn't simply increase his salary by the amount we were willing to pay. As a rule of thumb, parents should pay for anything they wish to keep under their control.

Q: What if you have a child who is so money hungry that he stops spending money at all and just sits at home all the time?

A: If you are going to trust your kids to participate in this kind of program, you must accept their decisions. Personally, I don't think this would go on for long, and you may be simply anticipating something that will never happen. For sure, there will be some extreme behaviors in the beginning. But they will level out. Keep a journal so you'll be able to remember the stories.

Q: I think it's too risky to give my son this kind of latitude. What if he takes all his money and buys cigarettes with it or worse?

A: If that is your worry, you have something other than a salary problem. Putting your kids on this kind of salary or an allowance program isn't going to create rebellious behavior. If that behavior is already in place, you need to deal with it before proceeding with this kind of plan.

Q: Isn't it a little rigid to say "no borrowing"? Kids are kids, and if they don't have enough money or forgot to bring it with them to the store, shouldn't we cut them a little slack?

A: I say no. The point of this program is to get your kids ready for the real world. You wouldn't want your twenty-five-year-old daughter thinking that every time she didn't have any money in her purse someone (Visa? MasterCard?) should cut her a little slack by giving her a loan, would you? Well, now's the time to teach that value. Your kids will not suffer long if they have to forgo an item they really want or sit home a time or two.

Q: What if the family goes out for a movie? Does the child on salary have to pay for his own ticket?

A: That all depends on what your plan says. You should address those kinds of issues ahead of time. And since you asked, I'll tell you what we did. If

195

we went to a movie for a family outing, we picked up the tab—it was our treat. And let me tell you that once your kids are on salary, they will really appreciate Mom and Dad buying a movie ticket.

Q: My daughter is sixteen and has never had any kind of consistent money training. She's never received an allowance, and I feel bad about that. Is it too late?

A: No! But you have no time to lose. I suggest you read this book through again and then have her read it.

This isn't difficult, especially for an older teen. I would start with a three-month plan. Set her up on a weekly allowance using chapter 15 as a guide. She'll pick it up quickly, and you can move right into a more aggressive salary program.

Q: We tried this kind of a plan with our eleven-year-old daughter, and it was a disaster. She spent all of her money foolishly in the first week. We held on for another week but decided she was just too young.

A: You can't expect your child to become a responsible money manager overnight. You have to stick with it. You cannot supplement with more cash when she makes mistakes.

You want her biggest financial bloopers to happen early on when there is no harm that can come to her while she suffers. You must let her face and feel the consequences of her choices.

Kids do learn eventually, and it's better that they do while they are at home and not a thousand miles away on a college campus with a credit card in tow.

Q: What about cars for teens? Who buys what?

A: No doubt about it, teens and cars go together these days. First there's the cost of the car, which is followed by insurance, gasoline, and maintenance. There are many things to consider.

Is this a want or a need?

What are the alternatives?

Is there a family car to share?

You might consider a matching program. Or if the teen buys the car, agree to pay for the insurance. Or vice versa.

Both of our boys saved enough money from the time they were about ten years old to buy a car in high school. We paid the insurance, but they covered all other expenses.

Whether your teens have their own cars or share the family's, they need to share significantly in the costs or there will be little appreciation.

Q: When should my son get a credit card, if ever?

A: I think the junior year in college is the ideal time, or when he turns twenty-one. (It really is necessary for every adult to have one credit card to use as a tool. Graduating college students will need to show an active credit report to rent an apartment or get a job. Employers and landlords look at a credit history as a character reference.)

By this time, a college student can get a credit card with very little problem. The good thing is that by this time your child has been debt-proofed. He will know exactly how to use that card as a tool, not as a noose with which to hang himself.

If your freshman is going away to college and you feel he must have a credit card just for your peace of mind, you have several options:

1. You can add his name to your card as an authorized user. Then set up an account online so you can monitor it as often as you need to between statements so you always know what's going on.

2. You can cosign with him on a card in his name but request that the statements come to your address. In this case, he will start his own credit history.

3. You can have him get his own secured credit card in his name. He will have to put up a security deposit of about three hundred dollars or more that will earn interest (this should be his money too). The statements go to him at school, and he is responsible for how he uses the card.

age ten through teen

Under this arrangement, your teen cannot go over the three-hundred-dollar limit. If he should for some reason—and fail to make the payment—the card issuer will take his three-hundred-dollar security deposit and close the account. If your child does well, the account can be converted to a regular unsecured account after a few years, and he can get his deposit back with interest.

I would go with the third option. This keeps his activity off your record and makes him responsible for his behavior.

epilogue

You may wonder what has become of our boys. Well, I will bring you up to date. I won't go on and on about how great they are. And what fine, responsible men they've become. And how proud we are of them.

Jeremy Hunt

Jeremy is now thirty-seven. His family salary ceased the end of the summer of 1992. He worked part-time during college and graduated from California State University Long Beach in 1997, debt-free and student-loan-free.

Jeremy got a credit card during his junior year of college. He reports that he uses it occasionally as a tool but has never paid a nickel's worth of interest. He continues to be an amazing saver and lives well below his means. At age twenty-five, Jeremy bought his first home.

Jeremy majored in film production and now owns his own full-service post-production facility specializing in visual effects for film, television, commercials, and music videos.

Josh Hunt

Josh is thirty-six. His salary ceased at the end of the summer of 1994. However, he had already secured a job, so he had a rather lucrative few months.

Josh graduated debt-free and student-loan-free from trade school in 1997 as a state-certified locksmith. Josh works in our family business, Debt-Proof Living.

Josh, too, is an amazing saver and is working on a fairly impressive investment portfolio. Josh got his first and only credit card at age twenty-five and bought his first home one year later. Josh lives below his means, and as a result, money has never been an issue or a problem.

In 2006, Josh married Wendy, and in 2009, Elijah was born, making Harold and me quite possibly the most obnoxious grandparents on earth.

Uncle Harvey

Uncle Harvey died in 1993. Not long after, his son Paul and his wife, Sandra, visited us in California. You can imagine how anxious I was to meet Uncle Harvey's youngest so we could compare notes. After all, Paul had grown up under the original Hunt Financial Program—the deluxe model from which we'd adapted our financial plan.

We were eager to share with Paul how we had customized his family's plan and passed it on through the lives of our sons. And you can believe I'd be taking notes. You just never know—maybe one day Paul and Sandra's kids would compare notes with our kids in order to help customize just the right plan for their kids. (Maybe they'd write a book.) We were about to experience a heritage moment.

I was nothing if not stunned when Paul responded to my opening question with a blank stare. The silence was deafening. Following what seemed like an eternity, he explained he'd never heard of such a thing, giving any kids—and certainly not him or his three brothers—all the money they would need for an entire year. All at once. In cash.

You could have knocked me over with a feather, and Harold would have fallen right behind.

I wasted little time writing to Aunt Rotha inquiring about the plan. I did feel bad questioning Paul's memory, but it crossed my mind that maybe they did things so smoothly, and Paul being the youngest, that he didn't realize he was on such a plan. It could happen.

Her response confirmed that Paul was right—we were way off base. The story we'd heard (and embellished beyond the legal limit I'm sure) was a legend, and not a very well-known one at that.

I couldn't believe it. We'd spent all those years shaping and designing our children's financial training only to learn that our inspiration was nothing more than a legend.

Aunt Rotha wrote, "Regarding the allowances given to our boys, they had their chores to do to earn it—chores at the barn, milking the cows, and sending the milk to the factory each day thus receiving a monthly check, which they divided among themselves."

It was a myth, an urban legend, but we quickly realized that it didn't matter. Not a bit. In fact, had we not believed the story, I doubt we would have had the courage to take it and expand, develop, and customize it to fit our family.

I'm thankful we didn't attempt to confirm the details at the beginning of our journey. Had we known we were making it up as we went, we might have doubted our ability to carry through. Because we believed the trail had already been blazed, we had the courage to follow.

Truly it was a journey of faith.

afterword

the letting-go part of parenting isn't easy. But we can make the process easier and much more enjoyable if we keep this thought at the front of our minds: God's plan is for children to grow wings and fly away.

Our job as parents is to prepare them for the flight. Building financial confidence in your kids is one important way you can help them fly high above the turbulence with grace and endurance.

I would love to hear from you to know how those flying lessons are going!

Mary Hunt

Debt-Proof Living

P.O. Box 2099

Cypress, CA 90630

Or online at DebtProofLiving.com

notes

Introduction

1. Third Women's Policy Research Conference Proceedings: Exploring the Quincentennial [part 43 of 90], Contemporary Women's Issues Database, January 1, 1994, 173–76.

2. "Growth in Bankruptcy Filings Slows in Calendar Year 2010," February 15, 2011, http://www.uscourts.gov/News/NewsView/11-02-15/Growth_in_Bankruptcy_Filings_Slows_In_Calendar_Year_2010.aspx.

3. Consumer Debt Statistics for 2010 from the Federal Reserve Bank, "Consumer Debt Statistics," http://www.money-zine.com/Financial-Planning/Debt-Consolidation/Consumer-Debt-Statistics/.

Chapter 1: Developing Financial Confidence

1. Public Law 111-24–May 22, 2009; Credit Card Accountability Responsibility and Disclosure Act of 2009; Title III—Protection of Young Consumers.

2. Tiffany Young, iMedia, "Kid-Directed Marketing," www.imediaconnection.com/content/8151.asp.

3. MasterCard US Ads and Offers, http://www.mastercard.us/ads-and-offers.html.

Chapter 7: Parenting—a Curious Profession

1. Charles R. Swindoll, *You and Your Child* (Nashville: Thomas Nelson, 1977), 27.

2. Gary Smalley, *The Key to Your Child's Heart* (Dallas: Word, 1996), 49–52.

Chapter 8: They're Coming after Your Kids

1. Federal Reserve Statistical Release, Consumer Credit, September 8, 2011, http://www.federalreserve.gov/Releases/g19/Current/.

2. Creditcards.com, specifically http://www.creditcards.com/credit-card-news/credit-card-industry-facts-personal-debt-statistics-1276.php.

3. Federal Reserve Bulletin, February 2009, A46, http://www.federalreserve.gov/pubs/bulletin/2009/pdf/scf09.pdf.

4. Robert D. Manning, *Credit Card Nation: The Consequences of America's Addiction to Credit* (New York: Basic Books, 2000), 159–94.

5. http://www.federalreserve.gov/boarddocs/rptcongress/creditcard/2011/downloads/ccap_2011.pdf.

6. The Associates National Bank of Delaware Visa® (now a part of Citibank).

7. "How Undergraduate Students Use Credit Cards: Sallie Mae's National Study of Usage Rates and Trends, 2009," http://images.bimedia.net/documents/SLMCreditCardUsageStudy41309FINAL.pdf.

8. Letter from Debt-Proof Living subscriber, Maureen M., Ohio.

9. Letter from Debt-Proof Living subscriber, Cyd B., Ohio.

10. Letter from Debt-Proof Living subscriber, Kay S., Colorado.

11. Letter from a college student, Ted K., Kansas.

12. Mary Pilon, "Students Still Targets of Credit-Card Offers," *Wall Street Journal*, January 8, 2011, http://online.wsj.com/article/SB10001424052748704030704576069611635998604.html.

13. http://www.getdebit.com/teen-debit-card/current-by-discover/.

14. Little Tikes Cozy Pumper, http://www.amazon.com/Little-Tikes-619991-Cozy-Pumper/dp/B003TPPXAU/ref=sr_1_2?s=toys-and-games&ie=UTF8&qid=1313001638&sr=1-2.

15. Cool Shoppin' Barbie, http://www.amazon.com/Mattel-17487-Cool-Shoppin-Barbie/dp/B000OY1Z7O/ref=sr_1_1?s=toys-and-games&ie=UTF8&qid=1313001236&sr=1-1.

16. Pretend & Play Calculator Cash Register, http://www.amazon.com/Learning-Resources-Pretend-Calculator-Register/dp/B00000DMD2/ref=sr_1_1?s=toys-and-games&ie=UTF8&qid=1313613972&sr=1-1.

17. Jump$tart Coalition, www.JumpStart.org.

18. Letter from Debt-Proof Living subscriber, Stephanie A., Missouri.

Chapter 9: Future Debtors of America

1. "Marketing to Kids," CBS News, 2007, http://www.cbsnews.com/stories/2007/05/14/fyi/main2798401.shtml.

2. National Institute on Media and the Family, "Children and Advertising Fact Sheet," www.MediaFamily.org.

3. Bruce Horovitz, "Marketing to Kids Gets More Savvy with New Technologies," *USA Today*, July 27, 2011, http://www.usatoday.com/money/industries/retail/2011-07-27-new-technolgies-for-marketing-to-kids_n.htm.

4. "The Power to Engage the Multi-Dimensional Teen," http://www.alloymarketing.com/media/teens/index.html.

5. James McNeal, "Poll of Children Shows Whining Wins," *Pittsburgh Post-Gazette*, June 17, 2002.

6. Jones Lang LaSalle, "Gen Y and the Future of Mall Retailing," http://www.us.am.joneslanglasalle.com/Lists/ExpertiseInAction/Attachments/255/JLL-Gen-Y-Mall-Retailing.pdf.

7. "How Teens Use Media: A Nielsen Report on the Myths and Realities of Teen Media Trends," 2009, http://blog.nielsen.com/nielsenwire/reports/nielsen_how teensusemedia_june09.pdf.

8. "ALC Targeted Data for Multi-Channel Campaigns: Marketing Teen Girls," www.alcdata.com.

9. Norman Herr, PhD, professor of science education, California State University, Northridge, "Television and Health," http://www.csun.edu/science/health/docs/tv&health.html.

10. Geraldine Lay Bourne, Nickelodeon Children's Television Network, quoted in "A Cable Challenger for PBS as King of the Preschool Hill," *New York Times*, March 21, 1994.

11. Kaiser Family Foundation, "Electronic Media in the Lives of Infants, Toddlers, and Preschoolers," the Henry J. Kaiser Family Foundation, Menlo Park, CA, 2003.

12. Ibid.

13. American Psychological Association (APA), "Television Advertising Leads to Unhealthy Habits in Children," 2004, http://www.apa.org/news/press/releases/2004/02/children-ads.aspx.

14. Mary Pipher, *The Shelter of Each Other* (New York: Putnam Adult, 1996), 89–90.

15. Channel One News, http://www.channelone.com/about/.

16. John Murray, "TV in the Class Room: News or Nikes?" *Fairness and Accuracy in Reporting*, http://www.fair.org/index.php?page=1565.

17. "Jump$tart Coalition 2008 Survey of Financial Literacy among High School Students," www.jumpstart.org/downloads24.html.

Chapter 12: Develop Financial Intelligence

1. http://www.kiplinger.com/magazine/archives/2005/02/millionaire7.html?kipad_id=2?kipad_id=2.

2. http://redaprons.com/kulynych.aspx.

3. http://money.ca.msn.com/small-business/gallery/gallery.aspx?cp-document id= 24458913&page=3.

4. http://www.fdic.gov/deposit/deposits/insured/basics.html.

5. Alvin Danenberg, *21 1/2 Easy Steps to Financial Security* (Chicago: International Publishing, 1995), 50. Reprinted with permission of the publisher.

6. Here is the calculator I used: http://www.globalrph.com/davesfv.htm. I put .01 in the first box, 0 in the second box, annual in the next box, 6 in the interest rate, and 520 in the years until retirement. Future value: 144,228,118,378.68.

index

Book Mary to speak at your next event

Over the past twenty years Mary has spoken at live events, conferences, seminars, and retreats across the United States and around the world. Here's what others are saying about Mary:

"We love when Mary comes to IWU, she always relates so well to our students."
—Chapel speaker and business school guest lecturer 2000, 2001, 2005, 2009, and 2011, Indiana Wesleyan University

"Thank you, Mary, for speaking at the 2008 Biennial Conference for Women. Your presentation was outstanding!"
—Biennial Conference for Women, 2008, University of Illinois Urbana-Champaign

"The key and strength of Mary's message is that people come away thinking they could actually do what she teaches! This is the very exciting part of her writing and speaking ministry."
—Pastors and Spouses Retreat, 2010, Canadian Conference of MB Churches

To book Mary or learn more about her, contact:

Cathy Hollenbeck
PO Box 2099
Paramount, CA 90723
(562) 630-6472
Cathy@DebtProofLiving.com
www.DebtProofLiving.com

What Is Debt-Proof Living?

It's a great big wonderful website offering help and hope to anyone who wants to learn how to manage their money more effectively. If you want to get out of debt—or stay out—and learn how to live below your means, Debt-Proof Living is the place to be. It encompasses many elements:

A lifestyle

Debt-proof living is a way of life where you spend less than you earn; you give and save consistently; your financial decisions are purposeful; you work toward your goals by following a specific plan.

A system of personal money management

Debt-proof living is a specific method that makes it possible to debt-proof your life.

A newsletter

In continuous publication since 1992, DPL newsletter is now published in an online format available to all members of this website.

A website

DebtProofLiving.com is the home of the debt-proof living brand. It is primarily a member-only website with features ranging from money management tools, articles, resources, community forums, consumer tips, recipes, and more.

Visit www.DebtProofLiving.com today!

These 7 simple rules will change your life!

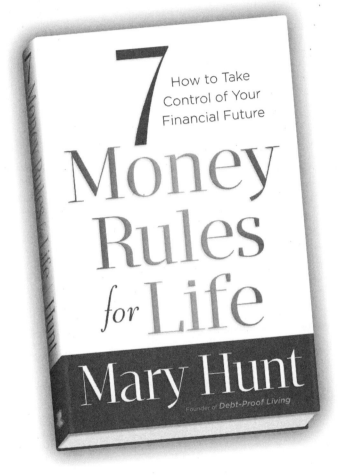

These days most of us need some help managing our money. Mary Hunt's simple rules will move you from financial uncertainty to financial confidence!

Ⓡ Revell
a division of Baker Publishing Group
www.RevellBooks.com

Available Wherever Books Are Sold
Also Available in Ebook Format

Be the First to Hear about Other New Books from Revell!

Sign up for announcements about new and upcoming titles at

www.revellbooks.com/signup

Follow us on **twitter**
RevellBooks

Join us on **facebook**
Revell

Don't miss out on our great reads!

Revell
a division of Baker Publishing Group
www.RevellBooks.com